My Mother – Myself

Ah, how quickly the hands on the clock circle toward the future we thought was far away! And how soon we become our mothers.

— Peggy Toney Horton, *Somewhere in Heaven My Mother is Smiling*

My Mother – Myself

GLIMPSES INTO THE COMPLICATED MOTHER-DAUGHTER RELATIONSHIP

Bobbie Spivey

Billie Ruth Furuichi

Edy Henderson

Editors

My Mother—Myself

Cover design by Billie Furuichi
Book interior design by River Sanctuary Graphic Arts

ISBN (Print version) 978-1-935914-58-7
ISBN (e-Book version) 978-1-935914-59-4

Printed in the United States of America

Additional copies available from:
www.riversanctuarypublishing.com

Library of Congress Catalog Number: 2015938412

RIVER SANCTUARY PUBLISHING
P.O. Box 1561
Felton, California 95018
www.riversanctuarypublishing.com
Dedicated to the awakening of the New Earth

FOREWORD

It began one summer as two of the editors were sitting around sharing stories. It was a simple thing like, "You won't believe what my mother just did!" that got them started.

Soon they were talking with their girlfriends – and it was suddenly apparent that everyone had some kind of mother issue they wanted to share. No one remembers whose idea it was – but one of them said, "We gotta write these stories down!"

Third editor comes on the scene, having a little experience with books and such; and the three of them have a weekend at Edy Henderson's home hashing out ideas. We all go off with great plans, encourage our friends to contribute stories, then armed with a scholarly proposal and a few sample stories, shopped around for an agent.

We actually had a few nibbles on our proposal, but "they" wanted to make changes to the focus – make it a humorous little book to carry around in a purse. We went through discouragement, renewed interest and encouragement and . . .

Eight years later – yeah, can you believe it? We awaken to the fact that self-publishing is not scowled on anymore. Not only that – but as we talk up the project to other women, we realize that the topic is still an exciting one – people simply want to know more about it. It takes little effort to solicit more contributions. Better still, we have interested buyers already reminding us to put them on our list when the book comes out.

Thank you to all those angels (like Linda Sivertsen and Lynne Klippel, Samantha Bennett and Ken Stone) who have continued to encourage us, to our writing groups (like *Sparks n Barks*) who lovingly critiqued and pointed out that we already had our subtitle. Thank you to those long-ago agents who responded to the first proposal and tried to send us in the right direction. Thank you – most of all – to those brave women who lent us a piece of their story so that we could include it in this book. We are feeling the blessings all around!

And – just last Christmas, we realized that there are "mother stories" that many of our men friends may wish to share – so this is an open invitation to all our readers . . .

~ If any of these stories strike a spark of memory for you

~ and you can't wait to share your own story

~ consider sharing it with us . . .

There's a second book on its way!

Contents

Chapter Three

EXPECTING TIME TO ALLOW US TO MAKE ADJUSTMENTS
Otherwise known as: *If I Had Only Known*

Chapter Four

REGRETS? PERHAPS – BUT THERE ARE NO DO-OVERS
Otherwise known as: *Letting Go*

INTRODUCTION

People throughout the world share stories of the turning points in their lives. Many of these stories percolated within the influence of a mother-child relationship. The actual decisive moment of those turning points may have been made on our own, but they were colored by an attempt to separate our lives from those of our mothers and to step out independently. This stepping out on our own, at each gateway of growth in our lives – is the leitmotif running through *My Mother – Myself*.

Working our way through one rite of passage in our lives does not guarantee that the next one will be easier. It is in sharing these moments with other women that we recognize the kinship and commonality which connect us, even when we are of different ethnicities, different social structures and different generations. It is that very commonality of our experiences which acknowledges the spiritual strands that weave us together as women.

My Mother – Myself is a compilation of real stories written by women from varied backgrounds and many levels of education. As we share stories about our mothers, our greatest and first love is revealed. And in that process we must also reveal our inner most selves. We were joined together when our eyes first linked;* and that link has bound and connected us all of our lives.

Every women has struggled with the ambivalence of becoming the archetypal mother we idolize, and of fighting against the taking on of her most bothersome behaviors. When we recognize that as an inner battle and begin to look deeply into ourselves, healing old wounds is truly possible. When we can accept our mother as an important icon in our life – and hope she can accept us as an adult with valid visions of our own – the final bridge can be built so that we might be able to

i

cross into each other's country and appreciate the beautiful landscape we have each created. For some of us this is possible, and for some of us it is important to accept that it is not.

We wish to include adopting mothers, as well.

Chapter One

"I Can Do It Myself, Mom— I'll Call If I Need You."

Otherwise Known As:

Leaving Home

> When I became a mother myself, I developed a self-righteous
> sense of superiority to my mother . . . By sheer force of will . . . I believed . . .
> I had skirted all that I might have inherited.
>
> —Katie Hafner, *Mother Daughter Me*

> I know there's something troubling you. I'm not going to ask what it is, if you
> don't want to tell me . . . But remember that I'm your mother. Nothing you say
> could ever shock me or make me love you less.
>
> —Erin Hunter, The Forgotten Warrior

That's what she'll tell you – but honestly, some of the things you've done on your own are not much to be proud about. But finding that first job, apartment, or car – and paid for by yourself – feels as if you can accomplish anything; you are on top of it all – Come on, World! Who needs a budget – I'm ready!

But are you really? You get a flat tire, you spill red wine on the carpet, you host your first dinner party and don't know how to make anything.

We all have flashes of needing independence – beginning during the "terrible twos." Those family rules are traditions you don't need anymore.

It is too much fun breaking out – the need for your own individuality – your own space is intoxicating . . .

Mom wants to buy something decent, modest, and you want to show some skin. You're busting out, you want to be the flower and have the bees come to you. Your mother, however, wants to lock you in the greenhouse.

Your wings are still damp, even as they grow stronger – yet you are eager to step to the edge of the nest. Flapping them sometimes pulls you off balance, yet as you teeter there, you know your essence demands that you step off and trust the wind will send an updraft.

Then you sense the underlying missing items in your personal arsenal. There is no "fall back" to fall back to.

MOTHER'S INTENTIONS

Nina Boyd Krebs

©2006

I couldn't help myself. Crushed garlic, cumin, (or *comino*, as Mother called it) and oregano sizzled in a tiny bit of oil, hurling their special home-cooking memories heavenward. After I added flour that bubbled in the light roux, I poured in a can of red chili sauce, completing Mother's classic enchilada sauce. Then, I had to run a little water in the can, rinse down the coating of chili that stuck inside, and drain water and chili rinsings into the pot. I couldn't simply rinse the can, toss it into the recycling, and forget it. The ritual wasn't complete without that final rinse, slosh, and pour.

Her ways of doing things were exact – and right. She had her reasons and they made sense.

"I made a dress that had a three-colored sash. When I sewed the colors, I stopped and changed the thread each time I started a new color," she had instructed me in one of those sewing lessons that had me wondering why I had ever asked. "I won first prize for that dress in a contest at school." She did sew beautifully, made lots of my clothes until I went to college, and I loved most of them.

And the scary part is that I stored the words and the images, but I don't have her patience or interest in perfection. I just think about how important it is not to waste food as I rinse out the chili can, and what a slob I am when I hurriedly complete some job that I know would never pass her inspection.

3

I still have some of her recipes. "FIELD STONE WINERY" the box's cover proclaims. Its wood has darkened with twenty years' sitting around. The "woodburned" portrait of the winery itself brings back the happy day Dave and I tasted there, excited not only by being together and sampling excellent wine, but by the information that "our winemaster is a woman!"

The box is stuffed with yellowing scraps of history, "From the kitchen of…" cards, newspaper and magazine bits, some ripped out, some neatly clipped, favorite recipes I had stored from my previous life, as far back as Betty Crocker handouts from high school home-ec.

I wasn't prepared for the tears that floated my contact lenses when I saw Mother's handwriting on the old furniture store stationery headed:

H. L. BOYD SUPPLY COMPANY

115 WEST THIRD STREET

WINSLOW, ARIZONA

A recipe for the heavy fruitcake I loved, "Yummy Cake," flawlessly scripted on now age-fragile paper, topped the clutter in the box.

Mother's approach to fruitcake started around Thanksgiving with a meticulously assembled list and a mission to the grocery to buy assorted nuts, candied cherries, orange peel, citron, and other ingredients. The ritual rolled into full gear when she accurately measured each spice, sifted the flour twice, and stirred the batter. Lined-up loaves received strategically placed red and green cherries, to be circled by wheels of pecan halves, then moved to the oven. She baked them long and slow. Fragrant and cooled, they were clothed in aluminum foil, cuddled by a cheesecloth inner lining. Thirstily, the cakes guzzled their weekly anointing of blackberry brandy, until Christmastime.

Recipes for Hot Fudge Sauce for ice cream and Chili con Queso – opening its list of ingredients with "2 lbs. Velveeta Cheese" – nestled among other assorted treats. All of them feature loads of fat and sugar that I lust after from time to time, but don't cook.

When I saw Mother's handwriting on the grease-spotted store stationery, I could feel her warm intentions in sharing this woman-knowledge with me. Nourishment. Sweets for the impoverished, but unacknowledged, soul. Hers? Mine? I still plan my days around lunch. I imitate her cooking sometimes, never without images of her and shadow stirrings about the gifts I've received from her as well as pain that must have echoed her own.

Her perfectionism impressed me early. For years I've battled stage fright that includes the same terror that struck me when I glanced up from reading to see MOTHER sitting in my first grade classroom. My heart had raced excitedly when Mrs. Savage called on me. I proudly took my place, standing at the front of the room by the heat register with some classmates, to read about Dick and Jane. At the sight of Mother sitting on one of the first grade chairs, I shrank into a twig of shivering timidity. I stumbled and bumbled through words I knew well, and sat down, crushed – a failure at age six.

Unlike Grandmother Burleson, she had no temperament. Mostly she stayed calm, or at least so it seemed to me.

She only let me see her visibly angry one time. And that wasn't at me, but I was scared anyway. We had returned home from some errand in the car. Rather than pulling into the driveway, she drove into the alley behind the house. During World War II, my parents had a "chicken ranch" on the outskirts of Winslow. Mother hatched baby chicks from fertile eggs in an incubator in the shed behind the house. Someone had built a small chicken wire pen, complete with a latch lock gate, in our backyard. The chicks were to spend their infancy in this "nursery" until they matured and could move to more challenging life in the country.

When we pulled into the back yard, she slammed the car to a stop, jerked open her door, and yelled, "Major, you son of a bitch!" She jumped out of the car, and started flailing at a neighbor's black cocker spaniel, who slowly but methodically shook the last of the chicks in his bloody jaws. Fluffy yellow bodies littered the red dust and gravel center of the chicken-wire circle.

Judy and I sobbed and screamed, "Our chickies! Our chickies!"

Rather than bawling her eyes out with us, which she surely must have felt like doing, she looked at us with a strained face and said, "These things happen. You don't have to get all upset."

Displeasing her wasn't an option. Judy and I wore starched and ironed dresses – "looked like little dolls," and needed to be careful not to get them dirty when we played. Even in the summertime, we wore coveralls over them when we accosted the backyard sandpile.

Laughter in our relationship, was rare. Standing in the kitchen, one evening when she still was taller than I, I watched her take a glass from the white steel cabinet and fill it with water. She used the water to wash down a pill. From my little girl perspective I could see her front teeth magnified through the bottom of the glass and distorted by the water. It tickled me. I told her they looked like horse teeth. She cried. I had hurt her making a joke. I learned to be careful. By fourth grade my feet were bigger than hers. "We could just get the boxes instead of buying shoes for you," she joked – and I was hurt. She walked with stiff legs and short steps on little high heels, but I never mentioned her gait, knowing it would not be funny.

In fifth grade, we had an assignment to write about a woman (or man, for the boys) we admired and hoped to be like. I scanned through my internal list and had a hard time getting started. Miss Sedlacek, who knew my mother, said so all the class could hear, "Nina, why don't you write about your mother? She would be a wonderful person to be like when you grow up." An invisible hand grasped my stomach, and I almost cried out.

"I think I'll write about my Aunt Edna," I replied. And I did, although I had only seen her once or twice that I could remember.

Mother, at age forty, suffered an aneurysm in her brain – a stroke, but nobody used the word. She was flown to Phoenix for treatment and stayed there several months. Judy and I lived with friends of the family for part of that time, and I think Meme stayed with us some. Daddy had to work, and didn't know how to cook. I became expert at making meatloaf and baked potatoes several times a week.

She recovered with no visible effects except thin scars on her neck – permanent reminders of incisions for inserting diagnostic dye. She never talked with us about what that experience was like for her. I felt like a bruiser around her, like I had to handle her with the same care I used to dust the fragile blown-glass deer that she treasured. I felt such relief when their little feet went "plink" on the mirror as I set them down, and I knew they had survived another week.

"Your mother is a wonderful woman," was the refrain I heard from her grownup friends. What did they see that I missed?

Who was this shadow woman who was proud of her sewing and cooking but didn't seem to enjoy it? What would she have enjoyed? How could she have been happy? Was it really that she married the wrong man, that she would rather have married Orville Downs as Aunt Edna told Judy and me years later? Or was it the loss of the first baby, a little boy born with a bad heart? Or was it the times? Or was it that her mother had failed her, too, and she had to make up for feeling worthless?

Fun, laughter, and cuddling strangled in the midst of concern about doing everything right or not bothering Daddy. Grownup fun was drinking and eating. Kid fun didn't visit often. Uproar, laughter, mud and confusion, noisy toys, avoided our house.

She talked about being "bull-headed," smart, and independent. In fact, she couldn't take care of herself. Her tone spoke disdain when she referred to "schoolteachers." She'd taught for a year and then married. Her pretend competence and slicing sarcasm took the longest for me to sort out. How could this competent woman be completely dependent on a man who drank himself into a stupor nearly every evening? I decided I would never be dependent on anybody.

When I think of her I see her standing up. No smile. I can hardly visualize her smiling. The look is more one of worry or inspection. I remember one coral colored dress she had. She made most of her dresses because she was hard to fit, under five feet tall and round at the middle. This one looked really nice on her. And she wore her silver bucking-bronco pin with a copper saddle and turquoise eye. I always liked that pin. It was wild and free, out of sync with the way I saw her. I knew she liked it. Maybe it touched a secret part of her that still lived inside.

First Job

Edy Henderson

©2006

My parents bought our first newly constructed home in a new subdivision in San Luis Obispo, California. They saved money on the home purchase by adding the finishing touches themselves after the contractor had complete all the structural work. Mother no doubt came up with this idea, as she prided herself in being "half Scotch" and she loved nothing more than saving money. She didn't work outside the home after she married, but my Dad said that from all the money Mom saved, they should be rich. Every member of the family was to pitch in and help with finishing the house. Dad was to build the garage out of lumber salvaged from his brother's business. Mom and my sisters and I were to paint the interior of the house.

Mom assigned tasks to each of us and impressed upon us the importance of doing a good job on these important tasks. I don't remember what rooms Mom or my older sisters Sylvia and Patty painted. I vividly remember that my job was to paint the baseboards in the bathroom. I took great pride in that job and I knew that nobody else but me could handle doing this job as well as I could. It was a very important job and it was all up to me. I needed no help from my Mom or from anyone else. I could do it all by myself. I was four years old.

To this day I remember the pride and satisfaction I felt on this, my very first job. With my paintbrush in my hand, I carefully reached down (not very far) and painted horizontally, making every effort to paint the base boards carefully. I tried not to spill paint on the floor or to get paint on the walls, which were taped with a thin strip of masking tape. It

9

seemed like very important hard work, and I knew I was the right person for this job. I was all alone in there, taking on this major responsibility by myself. I didn't need any help from anyone.

While I was painting, at one point my mother came running down the hall to see what was causing all the commotion. Now that I think about it, she probably had to climb down a ladder from painting the living room ceiling to get to me. She heard me yelling at the top of my lungs, "Damn, damn, damn!" while I was painting, and she was quite alarmed. To me, my language was appropriate and went with the job. You see, I had observed my father doing work on chores, and I thought that a required part of doing chores included very adamant use of this particular language.

Mother was a bit taken aback by my language, and she admonished me gently to not use those terms. Then Mother praised my work and told me what a good job I was doing on this important task.

Looking back on this experience now, and having the perspective of being a mother and a grandmother myself, I realize that Mom assigned me, her young four year old daughter, this low risk task just to keep me occupied and out of her hair while she and my older sisters painted the entire rest of the house. However, the way Mom made me feel about my first job instilled a pride and a work ethic in me that has lasted a lifetime.

Making Do

Ruth Owen Puchek

©2006

My first memories of my mother are wrapped into those of our homestead in Arkansas. It was in 1930, during the Great Depression; we had come across from Colorado in a rare Velie automobile. My Dad horse-traded that big Velie for a 40 acre homestead with a cow, a horse, a goat, some chickens, an old Model T and a big drafty house. Dad took the Model T back to Colorado looking for work, while Mom and we three kids stayed on the farm, keeping things together. By most standards of the time, we were pretty well off because we owned our land. We stayed in Arkansas for one long year, buoyed by Mom's daily prayers and her total commitment.

I was almost four years old and was expected to pitch in and pull my weight right along with my older brother and sister and our Mom. I do not remember any cozy nights by the fire with stories being shared. I just remember that miserably cold winter and the long and dismal grey days. Collecting the eggs from the chickens was one of my jobs. The stingy hens did not appreciate being handled early in the morning, but that was the only time I could collect the eggs. Many mornings they would peck my hands right through the old cotton gloves as I reached under their warm feathery bodies with cold, stiff fingers. I remember, too, that the water trough for the animals would be frozen over. My brother or Mom would have to chop through the ice with the ax so the animals could drink.

I have a vivid mental picture riding four astride – me in front of Mom, as the four of us took the horse down the road to the school house.

Maude was the best horse I have ever known because she would take us down to the school, return to help Mom plow the fields, then return to the school house to fetch my brother, sister and me home for supper. People do not often believe it, but it was true that sometimes Maude made that trip back and forth all on her own. Mom would unhitch her from the plow and slap her rump, saying, "Go get the kids, Maude," and off she would go.

I always thought Mom enrolled me in school at the age of four to get me out of her way. She said I was smart enough – but the scars are still there. They called it "teasin'" back then. But I was bullied. That one year in Arkansas still gives me nightmares. All Mom's prayers and healing ways just seemed to make me resent it and her more.

We all thought summer would bring some decent weather, but the only memories I have of that summer in Arkansas is picking berries in the woods so Mom could make jam – and begging her to fan me all night long because it was so hot I could not sleep. I am sure it was a hard year for Mom. I am sure that was the point when she simply had enough of Arkansas. Dad came with the Model T and we all piled in and returned to Colorado. I think we negotiated with some of the neighbors to trade the animals for traveling supplies and such. I do not recall being aware of the details, just grateful that we were returning to Colorado where we had family and friends.

I guess I always knew my mother was a strong woman. She and Dad had married late in life and she was "set in her ways," as some would say. She had been a secretary and a school teacher before they were married; Mom was twenty-five and Dad was thirty-eight. She even shared the story of when she first saw Dad on the platform of a train station. She was on the train, passing through, and said to herself, "That's my man, if I never have him." I guess he never had a chance. None of us did, if the truth were told. Mom somehow got her way in most everything.

In their sixties and seventies, Mom and Dad started building a home in the Colorado Rockies, as their Retirement place. They could have had it built for them, but they were both mucking around in cement and rock, hammering up sheetrock and paneling. Mom often embarrassed me by stopping at the side of the road on our way up to Indian Hills and picking up a discarded glove or something else she thought might be useful. Those gloves did come in handy as she became an expert stone mason by first building a retainer wall, a well house and then the stone foundation of the home.

Dad had continued to drive on these treks to the mountains from Denver until he lost control on the dirt road leaving Indian Hills one evening. The policeman who came to investigate took his driver's license away from him; and Mom and Dad were suddenly without transportation. At the age of sixty-five, having never driven a car, my mother asked me to take her to get her driver's license. "Mom!" I said. "You cannot drive!" Her reply was, "Oh yes I can! I have been driving in and out of the garage, and up and down the alley for about four months. I've read the book and I know I can do it." So, I took her down and, sure enough! She passed everything with flying colors. Tough old birds, both of them.

Dad died peacefully in his sleep, a few years later. He just decided to stop eating and "get on with it." My sister tells me Mom died peacefully in her sleep, too. I was not present for her passing. But I know she was stubborn enough to call on God for several days before then. I was there when she strongly advised the Lord that she was ready and He was taking His sweet time in answering.

I have a picture of her a couple of years after Dad passed on – after she moved to southern California – where she is smiling, sitting behind the wheel of a red convertible. I would like to believe she is still enjoying the warm breezes in her heavenly home. Bet she finds opportunities to tell the angels a thing or two.

Sewing Lessons

Bobbie Hopkins Spivey

©2006

I am convinced it all began with button boxes. You remember button boxes. They could be cigar boxes, or cookie tins, or sometimes a mason jar. But they were always full of the most curious things. And you could always find them at your grandmother's or your great aunt's homes. I am sure that I was still under three years old when I saw my first button box. I remember stringing each strange and wonderful find onto a blunt needle and thread. Some of them were square, with four holes; some were wooden and shaped like flowers or animals. Someone had threaded the needle and secured a button as an anchor at the bottom. It might have been my Great Grandma Owen, because I can see her room in my mind's peripheral and feel her braided rug beneath my mind's bottom and out-stretched legs. The room is darkened because the heavy drapes have been drawn. Granny Owen didn't like it too bright in her room. By that time, she had to have been in her eighties and may have had cataracts behind those silver wire-rimmed glasses.

Remembering Granny Owen brings with it the scent of peppermint. She would reach into almost any drawer in her home and pull out peppermint candy – round white disks with swirls of red starting at the center and radiating to the outside of the circle. They weren't wrapped separately in those days, and sometimes you could see a bit of thread or linen lint on one, before it was quickly whisked away. The sweet was always broken into small enough pieces for a toddler to suck without danger of choking.

I was twelve when she passed away in her sleep the day after her 95th birthday. I was old enough to go to her funeral and I think it was my choice to do so. But it made me avoid funerals for most of the rest of my life. I missed her son's, my own grandfather's funeral, another twelve years later. Everyone knew that I was 3,000 miles away and studying for finals to graduate college. But I could have asked for special circumstances and probably gotten it.

After Granny Owen's funeral, we were all invited back to Gran and Grandpa's home, where Granny had her apartment. After greeting and feeding everyone, the family was ushered into Granny's large efficiency apartment and asked to choose an item they would like to have in remembrance. I took my time and waited for the older relatives to make their choices. I first chose the table-top radio. I had wanted one of my own and our family could not fit it into the budget. When my turn came around again, my heart bumped in my chest. I realized that no one had chosen my most coveted thing. My voice was hesitant and breathy. Could I please have Granny's sewing basket? It was full of treasures like tiny silver scissors and shuttle bobbins that looked like silver butterfly cocoons. Scraps of fabric with pins laced through some of them in rows and others hit-and-miss. The button box went to Gran, her daughter-in-law. I was secretly pleased, because I knew that I would still be able to stir my fingers through those buttons any day I wanted to at Gran's house.

Aunt Opal was Granny's "baby" daughter. The family didn't speak much about how old Granny had been when her surprise child was born. But Aunt Opal was just about twelve years old when my mother was born. Technically, she was my mother's aunt. But everyone called her Aunt Opal, and I knew she belonged to me! Aunt Opal didn't have children of her own and often took me or my younger brother home with her for a day. There marvelous special things happened. She taught me how to make cookies and decorate the tops with raisins. Being left-handed, she was the first to recognize that I could be ambidextrous – and gently guided my use of my right hand. She taught me how to write my name in cursive even before I was three years old.

Aunt Opal taught me how to make doll clothes when I was convalescing from a long hospital stay at the age of four. She cut out the patterns and showed me how to take tiny stitches up one side and down the other, being sure that I leave the neck and sleeves opened. She was a marvel at the sewing machine. Our family didn't have much money when I was growing up, and Aunt Opal would often make pretty dresses for my baby sister and me. One Easter we had matching dresses, but with the pattern of flowers in a different color for each of us. One was blue and the other was yellow. My mother had the black and white photo tinted to show them off.

At Aunt Opal's house she kept a special coloring book just for me in the top drawer of her bureau in the living room. I was so proud of that coloring book because I didn't have to share it with my brother or sister, who couldn't or wouldn't stay within the lines. I learned from Aunt Opal how to outline a portion of the picture at a time, and lightly color within that outline. It was so beautiful and I loved that I had my own box of crayons at her house, that weren't getting broken or the tips flattened off.

One day, when I was eight or nine, I pulled the coloring book out and saw that someone else had colored a picture. I knew it wasn't my brother; it was too neat. But it wasn't my work. Aunt Opal finally admitted that she had allowed the neighbor girl to color in it. Then she sat me down and told me about helping others and why it was important to share. The neighbor girl was about my age, and lived in a very uncomfortable home. Her mother was often unavailable and the girl had to feed herself and take care of herself. It was two years before I met the girl, but by that time, Aunt Opal and Uncle Johnny had adopted her as their own. They made it official around my thirteenth birthday and I had the opportunity to have a sleep-over and meet her. For one summer, we were best of friends as I spent many days and nights at Aunt Opal's home. Thinking about it now, I can hear the grandfather clock in the living room. It had a soft low "tock" and a higher but still soft "tick." Lying on the living room couch, I tried to count the sounds and fall asleep. The muffled "bong" of the hour striking always jarred me awake, until I could count myself back to sleep. I've heard other grandfather clocks, and never have I heard one as "softly spoken" as this one was. Maybe Aunt Opal had muffled it in some way. I never did ask her about it.

Gran, Aunt Opal's sister-in-law, taught me to embroider and to crochet. I was able to master the back-stitch on a curve by the time I was eight. Crocheting was a bit harder, but I had the shell stitch down for doilies in about two days. Times together with Gran made these particular lessons special. We would talk about nothing. But it seems that I would come home with just a wonderful feeling of being especially loved and blessed.

Now Gran was the original recycling queen. In the 70's, she had a cottage industry crocheting sun hats, "rag" rugs and shopping bags for the ladies in her retirement community in Southern California. The best part about it was these were crocheted from running strips of plastic bread wrappers, or plastic supermarket sacks. She would cut a curling strip of continual plastic "yarn." and would send out a call to all her friends to save certain colors, when she had a commission for a special item. The pure white sacks went into a two-piece bikini that was a special order. Roman Meal Bread wrappers were especially colorful and it didn't matter if there had been writing on the wrapper or sack. It was incorporated into the pattern of the item being crocheted. I still have one of the shopping bags; they are indestructible!

Gran's efficient use of resources was simply who she was. I can remember back in the 50's when she had us stop on the way up to their mountain home so that she could pick up one lone glove that was lying on the side of the road. It didn't matter which hand it was for. She wore out gloves while laying the stone wall around the well house and near pasture. After placing the stone and rocking it to settle the cement around it, she would use the index finger to swipe the line with a smooth concave groove. As the fingers on the gloves wore off, she'd switch fingers to do the swipe. So any old glove would do the work. My husband told me once, after we'd been married for almost twenty years, that I could forget half of what Gran taught me, and I'd still be full of more knowledge than most people.

Function and form were expanded by Aunt Carol Jane, my father's sister. There is something about the style and simplicity of her creations that always amazed me. She could have been Martha Stewart because there wasn't anything she couldn't do around the house. One Christmas she made an apron for Mom that was a simple folded piece of fabric, stitched vertically two times, making three front pockets. I borrowed the idea and made several more for relatives. She also made table clothes with designed stitches so prettily that you didn't mind washing and ironing them for a festive table. While my daughter and I were visiting one year, she taught us a pattern of folded and tacked squares that made a flower design for a pillow cover. And just last year, with another visit to the Northwest, I learned a simple quilting pattern that is both fun and easy. I now have a grandson of my own and a built-in reason to make quilts.

With all these clever and creative women around, my mother didn't find a need to learn to sew. I can admire her, now, for realizing that she didn't have the sewing skills they did and developed her talents in other areas. But at the time I was taking sewing classes in junior high, I was ashamed that she didn't even know how to thread the sewing machine. We had acquired Granny Owen's beautiful old White treadle machine. Dad oiled it and set it up in the space beside the furnace. It was actually a good location, because I was able to work in secret, out of the way of all the goings-on in the family.

When I was thirteen, I took one of Mom's dresses from her closet and looked at the size. I selected a pattern that was a bit out of my comfort zone, and fabric that was unforgiving of mistakes; and I set about making a Mothers' Day dress for my mother. I held my breath when she opened the package and admired the dress. She said she couldn't tell that it had been handmade. Again, I stopped breathing as she tried it on. She was absolutely beautiful in that tucked pleated bodice, the gathered skirt with a hem in just the right place. She wore it to church that Sunday and bragged to everyone who complimented her that her daughter had made the white, dotted-Swiss shirtwaist dress. I don't believe I have been any more proud of anything else I have made than I was of that dress. All that was created without measurements; all done in secret, on Granny Owen's old White treadle. Mom and I were to have a rough and rugged time together for several years after that. But our Mothers' Day Moment was ground into our memories and we knew that love would endure.

How Girlie Black Met Boyer White

Artress Cornmesser

©2006

The greatest fear of every black family with teenaged girls in the midfifties was pregnancy. As soon as a girl reached the age of puberty, she was watched day and night, humiliated with calendar diaries, pad counts, and given extra work to discourage any desires except sleep. Families with only boys considered themselves lucky, above the worry and frustration of it all.

Girlie was in the middle of five boys and seven girls born to Mr. and Mrs. Black. One day she heard a lady say to her mother, "I sure don't envy you, honey. If I had seven girls to watch I'd kill myself!"

"Kill yourself?" Mrs. Black gasped. "But that would be the unpardonable sin, you would go to Hell."

"Oh, I'm sure God would understand," the lady said and laughed at her own joke.

Mrs. Black didn't think it so funny. Girlie noticed a certain tightening down of the rules after that conversation, as if her mother was trying to prove to her friend that she could do a job of raising her girls even superior to God himself.

At age sixteen, Girlie decided she'd had all she could take and began to devise a way to be free of her parents and the other old cronies in their church and neighborhood. Girlie Black got pregnant on purpose.

When Girlie told her parents that she was going to have a baby in seven months, Mrs. Black fainted. She had worked so hard getting her large family to California and into good schools, and trying to make each one perfect, that the news of failure was just too much for her.

Toward the end of her third month, while the other children were in school, Mr. Black drove Girlie and all her possessions thirty-five miles away to a town where no one had ever heard of the Black family.

Freedom was a one-bedroom apartment in a large housing project with one bed, two blankets, one pillow, two plates, two cups, a little Naugahyde couch and rocker, and a welfare check on the first of every month.

Loneliness and the baby in her belly were so real, she cried herself to sleep every night.

Girlie cried when she didn't even know she was crying. One hot day while washing her two bed sheets at the housing project Laundromat, a little old lady (Girlie thought she must be at least forty-five) offered Girlie a piece of advice: "Honey, I don't know what you're crying about but if you're making a baby, it ain't gonna be worth it in the end, cause a baby will come here just like you make it and believe me a crying, colicky baby that never sleeps is no fun."

That same day, Girlie learned where the town library was located, and walked the six miles round trip for two months. It was a relief to read in a quiet place that always had the air conditioner on. She stayed as long as there was daylight. Initially, Girlie picked the easy books: romance, mystery for teens, poems by Dorothy Parker, anything by Erma Bombeck, or Ann Landers. Then, bored, she moved on to the classics: Hemingway, Leo Tolstoy, William Faulkner, Mark Twain, Herman Wouk, D.H. Lawrence, John Steinbeck, and others, leaving the library in time to lock herself into the cinder block apartment just before dark.

April brought three changes to Girlie's life. First, the Southern California temperatures soared to 100 degrees, too hot to make the long treks downtown to the library. Then, she felt the baby kick her in the ribs, a new and frightening experience. While trying to decide if she should go to the clinic, Girlie had her first visitor.

The knock on her little screen door was startling. Girlie was so happy to see her oldest sister standing there, she fell into her arms and cried five full minutes.

"I can't stay but a minute. Mama would have a fit if she knew I came over here, I'm supposed to be in school."

"Oh, I'm so glad you came," Girlie blubbered. "This baby is kicking me and I don't know what to do."

"It's suppose to be kicking, silly. You're five months along and he is just exercising his muscles, getting ready to come out in four more months. Anyway, that's one reason why I came over here, to give you some advice. I don't know what your plans are about dating and stuff but you need to be very careful Girlie. Since your bell is rung and you can't un-ring it, boys will think you easy and try to use you. Don't believe anything they say. That's all I came to tell you and to bring these psychology magazines from school for you to read."

Girlie was incredulous. "I don't date, Sister! A man at the super-market tried to talk to me but I pretended not to hear him. Aside from getting myself like this, (she laid a hand on her belly) I don't know anything about men. Boys either. And where in the world would I go *looking like this?*"

"Well, OK, just so you know. Be very careful and be selfish. Mama might let you come back home after all this is over. Everybody misses you, Girlie." And she was gone.

The temperatures in June went higher every week. Degrees of over 100 were the average any given day. Girlie was reading inside with her screen locked and the door ajar, hoping to catch the tail end of a breeze, when she heard the knock. Thinking it was her sister again, Girlie ran to the door with the magazine still in her hand. It was not her sister.

"Hi, Mrs. Black, my name is Boyer White, your mailman, I have a package that you need to sign for."

Unlocking the little screen door, Girlie stared at the box. In the upper left corner was her mother's name. "Oh, this is from my mother," she grinned. "Looks like she sent me a pair of shoes!"

"Well, open it to be sure nothing is broken. If anything is wrong you can put in a claim because this package is insured."

Girlie ripped the package open while the mailman looked on. "A radio! A real radio," she cried in amazement.

"Plug it in to be sure it works," urged the mailman.

Her happiness was contagious and Boyer White cheered along with Girlie when the first music notes floated from the little RCA Victor. "OK, it seems to be alright, Mrs. Black, you can sign here."

Girlie put her magazine under the flimsy piece of paper for support and signed her name.

"What are you reading, Mrs. Black, a psychology magazine? Do you go to Valley College? I've never seen you there and I go four days a week."

"Get real," Girlie sneered. "How could I go to college pregnant like this? Besides I haven't finished high school yet. My sister brought me these magazines from Loma Linda Medical School where she is going to be a nurse."

"Oh, I see," he said, looking at her closely. "Since you're reading them, let me know what you think of Jung, he's the hot topic of conversation at Valley. Half the student body disagrees with his theory. It would be interesting to get your take on him."

"Well, I haven't read all the articles and I'm not smart enough to argue with the guy, but I can tell you that I love his style of writing. Jung paints pictures with words that even I can understand. I want to write like that someday, when I grow up."

"When you grow up?" Boyer White said. "You sure look grown-up to me."

"Well, I'm not!" Girlie Black snapped. "As soon as I correct this mistake that I made, I'll probably be going home and back to school."

"Why waste time, Mrs. Black? You could go to Valley now, they would let you in. There are a few pregnant girls in some of my classes. No one cares and you shouldn't call your baby a mistake, it's – – "

Just then an angry voice from down the street split the air. "*You send that damn mailman on down here with my check, Girlie. I got a bus to catch!*"

Girlie didn't see Boyer White again until the fourth of July. When she answered the door he was clutching a thick yellow legal tablet, three #2 sharpened pencils, some hand written notes and a good-sized box from the Harris Company.

"What are you doing here?" She was surprised and puzzled. "This is a holiday, there's no mail."

"I'm not on duty today but I really need to see you. Please let me in, Miss Black."

Girlie unlocked the door, happy to have company on such a big holiday. Settling himself on the little couch, Boyer White began his story.

"I have been on staff of our school newspaper all year; now I have been called to active duty for the Army. What I need most is you to help me write my byline for the next three papers. I have all the notes right here," he held up a fistful of hand written notes. "Members of the school paper are having a bar-b-que tomorrow and it's imperative that we go. Please don't shake your head and say you have nothing to wear," he held the fancily wrapped package out to her. "This should fit you nicely."

Girlie opened the box to find a size 12 paisley maternity smock with a white Peter Pan collar. It was the most beautiful piece of clothing she had ever seen. She clutched it to her chest and said, "I can't go anywhere with you, Mr. White, I'm a pregnant Black girl, what would people think?"

"Let 'em think what they wanna, I need you," he snapped.

With her new smock on and her hair fixed, Boyer White told Girlie that she was beautiful, but the college kids were less than kind. One student cornered Girlie, looked at her stomach and asked point blank, "Who the hell *are* you?"

Never at a loss for words, Girlie shot back, "A human being, which is more than I can say for your ass!"

Instinctively, and in spite of Boyer's encouragement, Girlie knew she would never be accepted into the tight circle of college kids and agreed to write the column, signing it in his name. The ploy worked well and no one was the wiser.

One week later, Boyer White checked out of school, quit his part time job as mail carrier and went to Fort Ord, California for the start of his six weeks of basic training. That same day, a man from the Bell

Telephone Company knocked on Girlie's door.

"What do you want?" she asked, puzzled. "I don't have a telephone."

"I know you don't, Mrs. White, but Mr. White paid to have one put in here so you got one now."

From that day on, Boyer White called every day at four PM like clockwork. He wanted to know how the newspaper article was coming along, how the baby was kicking and how Girlie was coping in general. One day Boyer told Girlie that he was sending her his allotment check. "I don't have anyone else to send it to," he said, when she protested, "and it's more than that little welfare check that you get so forget about refusing because it's already a done deal, besides we need that money for the baby."

We, did he just say *we*? Girlie Black thought Boyer White just might be out of his mind.

She needed someone to talk to about the situation, wished with all her heart for another visit from her wise sister. But no one came and except for Boyer she was friendless.

At the end of basic training, Boyer called, bubbling over with the news.

"Well, Babe, I made it and thinking about you everyday was the only thing that got me through. Can you believe out of the 23 guys in my platoon I was the only one who could type and do shorthand? Most of them are already headed for Viet Nam but the Army is keeping me here, giving me a little office to run because they say I have *skills*. I'm really happy about that though, because I'll be close enough to look out for you."

The labor pains started in the middle of the night. Thanking God and Boyer White for the telephone, Girlie grabbed her bag and called a taxi. She need not have hurried. The next afternoon she could still be heard screaming for her mother and swearing to the nurses that she would never get in this condition again. When the baby finally came, Girlie was delirious. Through a fog she heard the doctor say, "A fine boy – perfect in every way." Then she fell into a deep sleep.

Girlie woke up to the sound of Boyer's voice. Tears streaked his face and his blond hair was tousled. "Sorry I didn't make it in time, Girlie, but you did good, the baby is beautiful and I love you."

Girlie raised the bed to a sitting position. "Boyer, how did you get here?"

"When I called and you didn't answer the phone I knew you must be having the baby so I just walked to the highway and hitch-hiked. The first ride got me to Santa Maria, the second one brought me on in. Of course the Army uniform helped a lot."

Girlie couldn't believe her ears. "But won't you get in trouble for leaving without permission? Are you AWOL Boyer?"

"Yes," he shrugged his shoulders, "But I'll just go back and tell the Army that I went a little crazy. They won't lock me up for long because they need me to run that testing office. What are you going to name the baby?"

"I'm going to name him Black because that's *my* name," Girlie said.

"You can't do that, the kids will call him a bastard. I'll give him my name, Boyer White Junior."

"You can't do that, Boyer!" Girlie was shocked.

"And why in hell can't I? It's a perfectly good name. It's held me in good stead for twenty-one years."

"But what will people say?" Girlie wailed.

"Let 'em say whatever they want to. This is our life and we have a right to live it any way we damn well please. I have a two-week leave in October and I'm asking you to marry me then. Say yes because I already bought us a cute little house in Pacific Grove, near the ocean. You'll love it. I checked out the schools too – be a good place to raise our kids."

Without waiting for an answer, Boyer turned on his heels, marched up to the nurses' station and dropped his bomb.

"The Black baby's name will be Boyer White Junior," he said to the disbelieving stares of the hospital personnel. "Give me the birth certificate and I'll sign it now."

In October, of that year, Girlie Black and Boyer White were married in a civil ceremony that lasted 12 minutes. Girlie's mother, Mrs. Black, stood up in proud relief as the bride's Matron of Honor.

Theirs' is a solid union that has lasted 43 years, cemented with love, happiness, children and grandchildren. Only death will put it asunder!

Silent Conversations

Billie Ruth Hopkins Furuichi

©2014

"You must have some kind of character flaw," Mom said flatly, her dull and graying, eighty-three year old eyes no longer sparkling with zeal for life.

My eyes weren't so bright either. All they could do was fix on the floral pattern of Mom's terrycloth robe – the one with the tear at the top of the pocket pulled down on one side exposing threads of a hem, mended long ago. "Maybe so. I'm sorry, Mom."

"Why on earth didn't you tell me all this years ago?"

"It was just………you wouldn't have been able to handle it, Mom. Me neither. I can't even handle it now. I'm sorry."

"You're right. I'm glad you didn't tell me. I just wanted all my kids to be happy. And now look at you. Bud, too." Mom just shook her head. "At least he tells me what's going on with him and Susan and Felicia. I can't figure out why he stays with her."

"I thought you just said that you'd rather not know."

"It's different with Bud. He still needs me to help him reason out how to handle Susan and Felicia. Even though he doesn't listen to me most of the time."

"So why do it? He's the only one who can handle Felicia, Mom. You know that. So, let him do it and just back off. Especially if he doesn't even listen. You know Bud. He's going to pretend to listen and then go right ahead and do what he wants."

"As always. He tells me that's what Susan is always accusing him of, so I have to believe that's what he does. Both of you kids could have done so much more with your lives, and just look. What on earth happened? What did your Pop and I do wrong?"

"It's nothing you did, Mom. Or Dad. Don't blame yourself. I mean, I just never wanted you to find out about all that terrible stuff between me and Glynn. At least Bud tells you what's going on."

"I would really rather not know, Billie Ruth. I wish he would just keep it all to himself."

"Well, there you go."

The silent gap between them is filled by dialogue from The Days of Our Lives on TV – *My life with Glynn was just that bad.* "Glynn made me tell him stuff that, that…" I say after a few moments. "Living with Glynn for seventeen years – that was the real soap opera."

"What do you mean? What stuff?"

"Stuff. You know. Secrets. You don't want to know – even now, Mom. Forget it."

"Billie. I'm old. Nothing bothers me now."

"Just stuff we could share, he said. When we first got married, he said it would bring us closer together. Things. Things that no one else should know about – especially you and Dad. Glynn said it was for bonding, and we couldn't build a life together unless we shared secrets. Secrets would bond us together, you know."

"Good Grief, Billie. No, I don't know. I don't know what on earth you're talking about."

"I was only five, Mom! Dad would have killed me. Come on. I was only five."

"What are you talking about, Billie? I thought you said it was when you first got married."

"No, the secret I told him. I mean the secret I told him was about something that happened to me when I was five."

"Why didn't you tell me then – when you were five – I'm your mother. I love you. What on earth could you have done at five that you couldn't tell me? If you had told me, then it wouldn't have needed to be a secret between you and Glynn? You could have told me. I wouldn't have punished you – whatever it was."

"Dad would have."

"Oh, Billie." Mom's head and shoulders slump hard, as if she will never be able to sit up straight again.

"I don't know. I just couldn't. I felt so guilty and I thought Dad would kill me, so I just never said anything. I was only five, Mom."

"We were in Springfield when you were five. That's when you fell down the church stairs and almost died."

"Yeah. I remember. Do you remember a little girlfriend who lived down the block from us? When I went back to school, I refused to sit by that little girl again. I can still see myself sitting at those little tables and that little girl coming up wanting to sit by me and I just got up and walked away and wouldn't let her sit by me, and I would never go over to her house again, do you remember that?"

"After what happened? After you fell down the stairs?"

"No."

"Actually, I do remember you not wanting to play with some little girl, and I always wondered why. But you were just getting over the injury and I guess I just figured you had a lot on your little mind. We almost lost you, you know."

"I know. I remember falling down those stairs and watching that hatchet get closer and closer to me as I fell. That's another little movie in my head."

"You landed directly on it, right in the middle of your forehead. I thought for sure you were gone."

" I remember waking up on the couch and you were crying."

"Your dad refused to take you to a hospital."

"Even then?"

"He was just getting back into the Church and he was trying to play everything by the book. Quit smoking and drinking and everything."

"What a horrible little town that was."

"Remember the heat? We were only there a year, thank the Good Lord. Your dad got a good job in Denver the next year."

"Thank God I didn't have to grow up going to school with that terrible little girl."

"Where do you suppose she got the idea to do something so awful?"

"I think she probably heard her mom and dad through the bedroom door; her saying 'stick it in. Just stick it in,' and she just took it literally."

"But how would she know where…" Mom starts to giggle "….to sitck it?"

"Mom!" Billie burst out in laughter. They both started howling like Banshees. "It's not funny. Really, it's not, funny, Mom."

"I know, Dear. But it really kind of is," Mom's eyes are twinkling now.

"I don't know, Mom, we all do terrible things. I have no idea how I can forgive myself for most of it."

"Like what? You mean, there is more?"

"I remember having headaches really bad. I remember doing things."

"What things?"

"Things. Not very nice things. Like that poor little puppy."

"Oh my God, Billie, what are you talking about?"

"Okay, so It was really hot and I was walking to the neighbor's house across the street. They had a dog with new puppies. I went into the garage where the mother dog was and I picked up one of the puppies to see it. It was so soft and so cute, and I just suddenly wanted to hurt it."

"Why on earth would you want to hurt a puppy?"

"I have no idea, Mom. It was innocent like I was. I couldn't hurt that little girl, but I could hurt that little puppy."

"What did you do?"

"I took it out toward the street and there were two big oil barrels sitting out in the hot sun. I was just a little bit taller than they were. I remember thinking, 'if I put him on the barrel, he won't be able to jump off and he'll be just stuck there in the hot sun.'"

Mom's eyes narrow with horror, as if she can feel the pain. I can feel it, too. The ghastly thought of that poor puppy, haunting me.

"That barrel had to be hot, Billie. It was 110 degrees in the sun!"

"I know that now, but I guess I didn't think about it then. I just thought about hurting something that couldn't fight back."

"So what did you do?"

"Nothing. I just walked away and went home."

"My God, Billie. Did anyone ever find him and get him back to his mommy?"

"I have no idea. I hope so. I pray about it sometimes but I don't think God could ever forgive me for something that terrible."

Mom shook her head. "God may, but I can't see how you can ever forgive yourself."

They both just stare at the TV for the next five minutes without saying a word.

"You do have some kind of character flaw, Billie."

"Now, see, Mom, that's what I'm talking about. I should never tell you anything."

Chapter Two

PLEASE LET ME HELP – AND – I NEED YOU, BUT I DON'T WANT YOU TO KNOW HOW BADLY

OTHERWISE KNOWN AS

The Push-Pull

Mom was the best at everything, and you should never, ever suggest otherwise.
— Rick Riordan, *The Mark of Athena*

It is impossible for my mother to do even the simplest things for herself anymore so we do it together, get her dressed.
— Daphne Gottlieb, *Final Girl*

Perhaps one of the most uncomfortable lessons we learn is that we are a product of our environment, no matter how loudly we proclaim the denial. When faced with a familiar situation, we react in much the same way we watched our mother react. Did she remind herself to count to ten before she swatted your backside? How did your mother make it all seem so … if not, easy…at least 'do-able'?

When you're screaming your mother's words in your mother's voice, do you hear that little girl in your head saying, "When I have kids, I'll never say that to them."?

With all the good intentions to do a better job when you grow up, what happens to that resolve when chaos bursts forth.

But do you remember that picnic supper on the living room floor – and how your mother made the last of the fried potatoes and onions seem a special treat?

Now it is her turn to look for guidance. Can she turn to you, or is she too proud to ask for help? Your mother has needs of her own that she cannot handle by herself. The family expects you to step up, conveniently forgetting any discomfort that may have existed between the two of you.

Helping her out of bed, taking her full weight upon your shoulders, shuffling toward the bathroom, you pray for the physical strength, the emotional calmness and the mental clarity to do, to say and to be whatever is needed.

Burnt Toast

Kathe Kokolias

©2006

My mother – when she cooked at all – burned nearly everything she touched, starting with the breakfast toast. It wasn't her fault really. In her family she grew up as one of three sisters. My mother was assigned the duty of cleaning, while my Aunt Kay baked. Aunt Madeleine shopped and helped my grandmother prepare their favorite dinners: *moussaka*, *pastitsio*, and lamb stew with fresh green beans.

It's not as if my mother couldn't cook anything; she did learn to make creamy rice pudding and melt-in-your-mouth chocolate fudge, probably to beguile a boyfriend back in high school. But her true love was cleaning the house. She concocted her own recipes for secret cleaning formulas that could make a chandelier sparkle – humming to herself as she took apart each hanging crystal, happy in her work – as long as she wasn't interrupted and expected to cook a meal. My brother and I would come home from school starving and she'd glare at us. "You're hungry – again?" as if making us breakfast early that morning should have been enough. All day she snacked on Fanny Farmer's chocolates, her personal rocket fuel, as she zipped around the house washing floors, vacuuming, and polishing the furniture.

In the morning she couldn't clean. She had to feed us instead. My father would sit at the breakfast nook table, coffee cup in hand, reading the paper. His daily breakfast for most of his adult life, except when he was in the Marines, consisted of coffee and two slices of lightly buttered rye toast.

He stared at my mother hungrily as she ironed my skirt for school and talked with my grandmother on the telephone. Smoke rose from the toaster.

"Not again, Eleni!" he bellowed, using my mother's Greek name.

My grandmother had called to talk about last night's dream, and she and my mother were trying to make sense of it. I grew up thinking that the women in every family talked together each morning, sharing and interpreting their dreams – dreams that held as much credence as the morning news on WTRY.

"You dreamed of a knife," my mother was saying into the phone, "so that means a man is coming. Who could be coming to visit, Uncle Tim or some relative from Fitchburg?" Mom told my grandmother that she'd better start cooking something special, because someone was sure to ring the doorbell, suitcase in hand, just in time for dinner.

"Helen!" My father had switched back to English, his tone more insistent. "I have to leave in five minutes. Could I please have something to eat?"

Mom said a hasty goodbye to my grandmother, whispering that she'd call her back as soon as my father went out the door.

Maybe this explains why I've never enjoyed breakfast, even though I've learned it is the most important meal of the day. Each morning I struggle to consume something to fill the void, though nothing seems quite right. Nothing satisfies. I married a man who, unlike my mother, loves to cook and is good at it. His favorite meal to prepare is breakfast. His specialties range from fluffy French toast drizzled with Vermont maple syrup, to golden pancakes that he flips with the expertise of a graduate from the Culinary Institute, to opulent omelets oozing with onions, green peppers and melting Monterey Jack cheese. He even offers to wash the dishes. My friends marvel, "What a guy! Does he have a brother?

Don't get me wrong. I know I am lucky to have such a caring husband. But the truth is, sometimes all I really want for breakfast is a piece of my mother's burnt toast.

Mommy's Robe

Bobbie Hopkins Spivey

©2006

When I was little I liked Saturday evenings best of all. That was when I could take a long tub bath without anyone hurrying me out so someone else could use the tub. Then, fresh from the steamy bathroom I would jump onto the bed where Mommy would do the "rub and scrub" all over my body. Well, maybe it did not happen every Saturday. Maybe it was only once in a while. But my memories of those cozy rubdowns are still vivid.

Scrunching up close to Mommy on her bed, with the scent of shampoo and soap still warm in my nostrils, I would snuggle into her fluffy chenille robe and wait for our special time together to begin. It was my choice. I could ask her to read a story or to tell a story from her own childhood. I loved to hear about my mother's horse, Maude, who would take her to school, come back to the farm to work the fields, and return when school was out to bring her home. When I was a bit older, mother shared a story of her own twelve-year-old bravery in the face of a deranged, knife-wielding woman while Mommy was babysitting her younger siblings. Sometimes, I would ask for a repeated story, just to stay closer to that younger version of my mother. Mommy's arms would wrap around me and I'd wiggle even closer to her body, tucking my head so that my cheek was caressed by the soft chenille across her arms. While she spoke, I would trace the veins in her arms with my fingers, lightly following them until they disappeared into the chenille. The magic stayed with me all night long.

When I was in high school I would often come home for lunch and find my mother still in her ratty old bathrobe. Her hair would be tangled and her face would be mapped by wrinkled pillow marks. I was disgusted to think she had been in bed all morning. It wasn't as if she were tired from being overextended. Dad didn't want her to work outside the home. All of us kids were old enough to take care of ourselves. All she had to do was take care of the house and have supper on the table when Dad wanted it. And that bathrobe! It had faded to the point no one remembered the color it had been. Strings of chenille had been pulled out, so that vertical tracks of perfectly spaced holes covered most of the material. Why in the hell did she still have that robe.

I never asked her about it. I was too ashamed. Even when we were older and back in each other's good graces, it never came up in our wonderful moments of "remember when." By the time I was in my thirties and had experienced my own bout of depression with the boredom of life, it still did not seem timely to mention this period of malaise with my mother. And now, when I have a leisurely tub bath on a Saturday – while everyone is gone and I have the house to myself – I'll slather on the cherry-almond scented hand lotion my mother favored; and I'll put on a set of comfy sweats and cuddle up to the current book I'm reading.

Sometimes, I'll stretch out my arms and recognize their similarity. The tiny lines that criss-cross between the hair follicles create a tapestry so familiar that I am pulled backward in time. I close my eyes, inhaling the cherry-almond fragrance. And KNOW that if I opened my eyes, I would see the fluffy loops of chenille unfurling down the length of my mother's arm.

July Fourth

Edy Henderson

©2006

Maggie and I walked briskly down the hill, enjoying the fresh air and exploring the sounds and smells of the neighborhood. She'd waited patiently for me to muster up the energy, nudged me and looked at me intently with large pleading brown eyes. She even vocalized a single soft bark. At last I could feel my energy rising enough to face the world again. Outside it sounded like Baghdad must sound. I wonder if Iraqis ever get used to the sound of whistling rockets, booms, and bangs. Tonight we're hearing the sound of Freedom's celebration. Santa Cruz has zero tolerance for fireworks, and those who dare celebrate freedom this July Fourth do so at risk, facing the full force of the law. It is not yet dark, and no flashes of light are visible. I can imagine in a few hours the sky will light up with "bombs bursting in air." I will watch from the deck to see fireworks from the beaches. This is the quietest Fourth of July I can remember at my house. No friends came by. They didn't know if I would be back home, or under what conditions. I returned last night from my latest trip to visit Mom in Oregon, a trip that lasted a very intense ten days.

The phone call came in on Fathers Day while we were driving to a baseball game with Marlene and Alonzo. Norma, told me, "Your Mother is seriously diminished. You need to come right away. She can no longer walk or feed herself and she is sleeping most of the time. This is a new stage of being elderly. After all, she is ninety-four. I'll be shocked if she pops back from this. You need to come soon. I fear this is the end." I replied, "Norma, you know Mom has popped back before." I told Norma I would book a flight for early in the morning.

The previous day Norma called 911 and the paramedics carried Mother on a stretcher to the ambulance. Mother had stopped walking and eating and was in such pain that she yelled every time she was lightly touched on her skin. A complete battery of tests found nothing physically wrong other than "continuing damage from previous strokes." The hospital said there was "no physical illness that they could treat." They tracked down her nighttime caregiver, and sent Mom home against my pleading.

My daughter Marlene was willing to take time off work to care for her Nana. I flew from San Jose the next morning. Marlene and her son Alonzo flew from Oakland and met me in Portland. I earn a lot of frequent flyer miles visiting Mom, although she and Dad were native Californians. Thirty years ago Mom said, "We've raised you three girls, now we have our own lives to live." They traveled, did missionary work in Japan, and settled in Oregon where they celebrated their 50th wedding anniversary. Mom is widowed now.

When we arrived at the Bible Students Retirement Center, Mom was barely moving in bed. What a change since my visit Memorial Day weekend! Norma was near panic because Mother had not recognized her that morning. In five years of caring for Mother, this had never happened before. When Mom heard little Alonzo's voice, she smiled for the first time in days.

I called the Kaiser caseworker. She arrived with a Hospice nurse, performed an in-home evaluation, and admitted Mother immediately to Hospice. The nurse reviewed Mom's medicines and found she had been taking mega-doses of painkillers, heart medicine, vitamins, calcium, sleeping pills, and Fosamax. Mother could no longer swallow pills or solid food. The nurses removed all the pills from the medicine boxes. Most of her medicines went down the toilet (remind me to sponsor a bill making this illegal!!). Mother was put on the bare essential medicines that we crushed and added to spoonfuls of ice cream and hand fed her.

Hospice sent a portable potty and a hospital bed that was wheeled into Mom's bedroom and placed next to her bed. My sister Patty arrived from California, and we now had three strong women and a five year old. We called the office and requested another able-bodied person. "Little Sharon" the LPN joined us and directed our next move. We each stood at a corner of Mother's bed, grabbed a corner of the sheet, and on the count of three, lifted Mother onto the hospital bed. We moved Mother's own bed to the garage. Mother barely reacted while we moved her.

I could empathize with Mother's helplessness, recalling the time I became bedridden with cancer. Mother had come to my aid. She always nurtured us when we were sick. At the time I wondered if I would ever recover, and set a goal to outlive my parents, believing the goal would inspire my immune system. Now, our roles had totally reversed and it was my turn to nurture my mother.

The hospital bed helped with lifting Mom into a sitting position for the lift and pivot. Once when I pushed the button to raise the head of her bed, she screamed, "Don't make me go up to the top of the curtain. I'll hit my head on the ceiling."

On the side table I found the new shoes I had ordered for Mom, still unopened. I figured she would never walk again, and planned to return them to the Post Office. Somehow I never found the time. Between phone calls and meetings with nurses, caregivers, visitors, and relatives I was on call every time Mom needed something. After a few days, I realized I was not going home soon. I called the local pharmacy and had my own prescriptions transferred to Oregon.

Mother could not move or control her legs or arms, and she could barely open her mouth. However, there was part of her body over which she had total control. She would not use the Depends we had bought her. Every time she had to "go", she panicked, called for help, and insisted on using the toilet. This required two able bodied people to sit her up in bed, gently pull her legs over the side of the bed, pull all of her weight up to a standing position, pivot her body toward the portable potty, and sit her down on the potty. All this was done while she screamed and wailed aloud for fear of falling. Mother is no small woman. Many caregivers and relatives decided their backs could not take the lifting. Marlene and I became quite adept at the "lift and pivot" maneuvers. Sharon taught us to explain every move to Mother and to reassure her verbally. Mark arrived from New Orleans and helped out, although Mother retained her modesty around her grandson.

The doorbell rang often. Some well-meaning neighbor gave words of encouragement such as, "Don't prolong things, Dear," or "I don't think she'll live very long, do you?" My standard reply became, "Only the Lord knows. It's all up to the Lord, not up to us." That reply usually succeeded in terminating the conversation in a timely manner. Then Sister Shirley came to call, bearing nothing but unconditional love, hugs, smiles and toys for the child."

My days were spent between "lift and pivots", hand feeding Mother, and meetings with nurses and caregivers to plan for her new level of care. One day we had a young strong caregiver who could handle the "lift and pivot" by herself and we took a one and a half hour break. Marlene, Alonzo and I went to the park. On the way, Alonzo expressed, "It's all about Nana-Nana."

My little grandson Alonzo decided that no one could be admitted to see his Nana-Nana without a password. He stretched his little arms to block the passageway into Mom's room. It didn't matter who came: it could be an RN, a church Elder, a ninety year old neighbor, his mother, or anyone. The rule applied to all: no password, no entrance. To enter, one had to say, "Joe Joe and Grace." And, he required a separate password to leave the room: "Joe Joe out of here." With a twinkle in his eyes, he held everyone fast to the rule.

On Saturday, our sixth day taking care of Mom, Sylvia arrived for the first time in sixteen years. Mother now had her three daughters, two of her grandchildren and one great-grandson all together. Sister Doris, mother's eighty-nine-year-old neighbor came to call. She embraced Sylvia and said, "I remember you from when you were a teenager." Sylvia beamed and returned the hug.

We told Mother that her other granddaughter Linda would arrive the next day with great-grandchild and namesake, five year old Gracie. We worried that Linda and Gracie might arrive too late.

That Saturday evening (the fifth anniversary of my father Homer's death), Mother stopped eating, and forgot how to swallow. She would no longer take in liquids. She babbled incoherently, and motioned to Homer's picture, as if to say she would see him soon. We kissed Mom good night and didn't expect to see her alive in the morning. We left her with Kay, the nighttime caregiver who was the only person capable enough to handle Mom by herself, and went to get sleep. It had been nine days since Mom had walked or fed herself.

I arrived with trepidation the next morning at 6:45 AM to debrief with Kay. She stood feeding Mother applesauce with meds. Kay said, "Grace, look who's here!" Mother excitedly asked, "Sylvia?" I moved into her field of vision and said, "Good Morning Mom, it's me, Edy." She replied with a flat, "Oh."

When I told Sylvia about this conversation, she said, "Wow, how does that make you feel? Here you do all the work, and I show up and get all the attention and credit. I guess I'm the prodigal daughter."

Later that morning Mark and Sylvia went to pick up Linda and Gracie. Marlene and I did the "lift and pivot" onto the potty, repeated the process into the wheel chair and wheeled Mother into the living room. I held her feet up while Marlene wheeled the chair. Again we did the "lift and pivot" into the recliner. We thought a change of position would help prevent bedsores. Mom slept in the recliner.

When Linda and little Gracie arrived with Sylvia and Mark, Mother woke up, opened her eyes, smiled, and said, "Hi, how are you? Welcome to my house. Can you stay for some chicken dinner? We forgot the rolls so someone has to go to the store to get the rolls and jam."

We all dropped our jaws and starred! Linda said, "What's the deal? Nana hasn't changed since last Christmas. She seems perfectly normal to me."

Mark was hungry and found some grapes. Mother looked up and said, "Aren't the grapes good this time of year?" Mark asked if she wanted some. She said, "Yes." Mark cut some grapes into pieces in a small bowl and was getting ready to hand feed her, when Mother reached into the bowl, picked up a grape, put it in her mouth, and ate it. We all stared and gasped in disbelief. Mother started laughing joyously. We stood around her chair and had a family picture taken.

The five year old cousins soon discovered mud puddles outside in the rain. Barefoot, they giggled as they danced and jumped into each puddle.

The next morning, the phone rang. Mother reached over, answered the phone and held quite a conversation. It was the Speech Therapist calling to arrange a swallow test. The Speech Therapist, wondering why she had been called, cancelled her visit. I decided to try the shoes on Mother. If they didn't fit I would take them to the Post Office. They fit perfectly, and the baby blue color matched her eyes and her wardrobe. When the Physical Therapist arrived, still wearing the shoes, Mother stood up with assistance, and walked for the first time in eleven days. Sharon, the LPN, almost dropped her teeth when she saw Mother walking, talking and eating. The look on her face was priceless.

I asked Mom how she was feeling. She said, "I'm better today, but I don't feel like running any races." Then she told her story. "They used to call me the fastest girl in three counties. Ha Ha Ha. I never ran long distances, but I beat everyone else in sprints at all the track meets. Once my brother Everett saw me run at College of the Pacific and he said, 'That's my sister.' One time Leland Stanford sent a car and rode with us up to a track meet in Northern California. He supported girl's athletics. I was the Commissioner of Girl's Athletics in High School. I played basketball and I ran track and I was voted the Most Valuable Player in both High School and College. The best thing I got out of college was your Dad, Homer." Mom was clearly back!

The nurses speculated that Mom had suffered another stroke, hidden in the MRI by previous stroke damage. A clot might be moving around in her brain, depressing different functions as it moved to different sections of the brain. The caregivers thought that Mom had been overdosed on medication. Each time Mom had complained, the nurse had called the doctor, who prescribed yet another pill.

Now that Mom seemed OK, the family began to disperse. Everyone else had caught a train or a plane to return home. It was hard to leave Mom, not knowing if we would see her again. We reminded ourselves that it had been Mom's choice to leave California and move to Oregon to be near her church friends. It was becoming critical for my own health for me to take a break. My lower back was feeling the "lift and pivots." The next evening after negotiating a new schedule with the caregivers, printing out and distributing a new caregiver schedule, I returned home as well.

A few days later, Mom accused the caregivers of stealing her bed. Mom insisted on getting her own bed back in her bedroom, and we called Hospice to have them pick up the Hospital bed.

Mom used her walker to go from her apartment over to lunch in the big house the next day. Heads turned and tongues wagged when they saw her coming, as if they were seeing a ghost.

Norma was shocked.

Mom called me today to tell me that she had talked to Sylvia on the phone. She sounded very happy!

Mom will be ninety-five in February. I still have a goal to out live her.*

Maggie and I are almost home now. It is getting dark and I see many colors of fireworks coming from the beach. Let's hear it for the celebration of Freedom!

*EDITORS' NOTE: Grace passed away a few months after Edy wrote this piece, and Edy lived an additional six years. Her goal was accomplished.

Vanity, Thy Name Is Mother

Charla Rotter

©2006

Mother was looking like a Hollywood celebrity when I picked her up to go shopping. From her impeccably manicured nails to her coiffed hair and her perfect mascara, she radiated glamour all over. "Just a minute," she called to me as she turned around and went back in the front door. When she returned a few seconds later, she was slipping her arms into her beautiful mink jacket. "Now, let's go wow them dead," she said.

Mom always taught me how to do everything first class. She was never ordinary, and never wanted me to be ordinary either. I know because she always nagged at me if my outfit was not perfect or if I had a hair out of place. She wanted me to be the perfect daughter of her perfect self. I guess I am grateful to her in retrospect, because I learned from her the value of striving for perfection in everything I do.

I drove us towards the back side of the mall and parked directly outside of Niemann Marcus. "OK, Mom, let's go get 'em," I said. She strutted into the store on her stiletto heels with her head held high in the air. *What a lady*, I thought. The Queen of England paled in comparison to her.

"Let's stop and try the new fragrances," she suggested, evading the perfume spray girl and opting instead to go directly to the counter to try the samples for herself.

I began browsing around looking for the best brand of lip gloss, testing the colors on my wrist. There were some new colors that I wanted to try, and I searched for the best shade to go with my new blouse.

From behind me I heard a sudden screech. Then I heard, "HELP! Help me Charla." My heart pounded as I feared the worst. I imagined Mom being snatched and dragged away by a strange man, or maybe having a terrible allergic reaction to some new chemical in the perfumes.

I turned around and ran toward Mom. And there she stood, covered with white foam as if she had just covered herself in whipped cream.

"MOM, What happened?" I called out. My horror turned to uncontrollable laughter as I saw her standing there with foam all over her new mink jacket. "Mom, what's going on?" I pleaded. Mom just stood there, with an expression on her face like a bad puppy who has just been caught peeing on the carpet.

"I don't know what happened," she said meekly. So I reached for the container in her hand and examined it.

"Mom, I said, trying to hold back laughter, "that's not perfume. That is men's shaving cream." I laid the container back down on the counter and tried to clean some of the foam off of Mom's jacket. The perfume girl and every other employee had disappeared. I had no tissues on me, so I tried to clean the foam off of her with my hands. I took a fistful of foam and shook it onto the counter, then wiped more foam off of Mom. Pretty soon we were both pretty much covered in the white stuff.

So much for looking like a million dollars!

I somehow found my way to the Women's Lounge, leading Mother by the hand. We washed the foam from our hands and faces, took damp paper towels and wiped off the mink jacket.

"Let's go and have high tea in the Rotunda," Mom pleaded.

"OK," I replied, "but Mom, next time you go to the perfume counter, please don't be so vain as to not wear your glasses. Remember what happened on our flight to Hawaii and you didn't wear your glasses?" Until next time the duo of Charla and Betty are on an adventure.

Help Less and Dig for Worms

Debra Madison

©2015

I am a first born; the first great-granddaughter, granddaughter, niece and oldest girl of our family of three girls and one boy. And I am a helper.

At 13 months old, when my brother was born, I helped my mother take care of him. Anything my mother needed, powder, diapers, bottles, rattles, and so forth, I would get for her. I happily helped and was praised for doing so. "Mommy's Little Helper" was who I was. My grandmas, aunts and uncles would tell me how sweet I was, what a good girl I was for helping, and how much they loved me. I knew that I was loved unconditionally, helping or not.

And boy, did I love my brother. Still do. He was my first friend. When I wasn't helping my mother, and had my brother all to myself, he became my real-life doll. Some of my favorite family photos are of my brother at around 6 months old in my doll's stroller, and me, leaning over him and kissing him on the top of his head.

Mom would take us on the buses in the Bronx, carrying my brother in her arms and holding my hand as we walked. I carried the diaper bag. She told me that I could barely get up the steps onto the bus at a year and a half, yet I did. She said that I was always very independent and strong willed.

When I was five years old, my sister was born. I can remember changing her diaper. I always helped. Mom never expected me to take care of my younger siblings, and I didn't. My job was to help my mother.

My job suddenly got bigger when my father unexpectedly died. He left behind a devastated wife, and three young children, ages eight, seven and three. I did all I could to help my mother. She was inconsolable as she wailed to the music she played on our record player. Sad melodies and love songs played endlessly, filling our once happy apartment with sorrow.

I stayed with her, standing by, doing my best to keep her from falling and sinking into greater sadness. My brother sat outside under a big tree in the grass and dug for worms. My sister waited on the sidewalks, with all the other kids, for our Daddy to return from work.

Eventually my mother remarried and my other sister was born. We all helped then, and some of the responsibility that I felt for taking care of, and helping my mother lifted.

It wasn't until many years later that I assumed the role of helper again. My stepfather had died, and six years after that, my mother's male companion died. She asked me for help. When she didn't ask, I inserted myself.

I saw her slipping, unable, or not wanting to make decisions. I became more and more involved in what she should do career wise. She would ask for input and then be resistant to everything I suggested. I started to feel resentful and frustrated. It was as if my mother sent out an SOS, I'd throw her a life jacket and she would push it away.

I sought counseling. I was drained, neglecting my own household and totally wrapped up in my mother's existence. I was asked, "Do you know how *not* to help?"

"Of course," I said. I was very much mistaken.

Intellectually, I understood my need to help and how it was impacting me in a negative way. I was even given the tools to help break the habit and pattern of helping. I still found myself helping to the point of my own exhaustion and detriment. It took years to learn and would take time to unlearn. Being aware was the starting point. I realized it was driven by the need to be needed, and the fear and anxiety about losing my mother. It had become habit. I was willing and able to take baby steps making small changes and making progress.

In August of 2013, my mother fell. The baby steps and any progress that I had made in my own life came to an abrupt halt. A compression fracture in her spine required a short stay at a Skilled Nursing Center. She excelled in physical therapy and rehab and went home after a 2 week stay.

It was a time when my mother did need help, not just from me, but from the entire family. My sisters, brother, two grown children their children, my niece and nephew, in-laws and close family friends all participated in caring for her when she returned home. I was afraid of her falling again and was willing to help with anything except for assisting her when she walked. Although she had a walker, and was regaining the strength in her legs, I didn't want her to fall again, especially on my watch. My brother, felt the same way. We were afraid of her falling, and felt that she needed professionals to assist her. Although my two sisters may have had the same fears, they put them aside and helped her as she moved about with her walker.

She recovered to the point of not needing someone there during the night and was able to be on her own and do more for herself. We were grateful. The compression fracture would probably take a few months to fully heal. She would be monitored with check-ups by her doctor and imaging of the area that had taken the impact of the fall.

Then in September, a follow-up scan of her spine showed something new. She had several tumors on her liver. The rest of the month was filled with a lot of medical appointments. After several types of more detailed scans and a biopsy of the liver tumors, it was confirmed. My mother had cancer. An appointment with an oncologist was set for the end of October.

The first week of October, while racing to answer the front door, my mother fell again. Her walker had slipped out from under her. She insisted she was fine and did not want to be seen in emergency or by her doctor. Four days later she was having terrible pain. We took her to emergency and she was admitted.

After a week or so, she returned to the Skills Center for physical therapy, occupational therapy and rehab. It took longer this time. My mother's spirits were low and she really disliked having to ask for help in and out of bed to use the bathroom, and having to be in a wheelchair instead of her walker. Most times she wouldn't request help from the staff and would want us to assist her. When we weren't there she was not asking at all, and moving about on her own. She knew that she was considered a "fall risk," it was important for her to have help.

Once again, I was afraid to help her in and out of bed. I would plead with her to have someone who knew how to assist her do it. We even argued one night as I was leaving. "Please ring the bell if you need to get out of the bed Mom, okay?" She wouldn't say yes.

Her appointment with the oncologist confirmed what was already suspected. Mom did have cancer, and it was very advanced. Her prognosis was not good, maybe 6 months to a year. The doctor stressed the importance of having trained medical staff to take care of my mother, rather than relying on family. Yes, she needed her children, grandchildren and great grandchildren visiting and spending as much time as we could with her, but when it came to actual care-giving and caretaking, he said it would be best to get professionals. It was a matter of safety. He also said another fall could be devastating for her.

We found an Assisted Living Community that my mother really liked. It was located close to the family, had lots of activities, she liked the food and the staff was caring and professional. The apartment looked out onto a green grassy area with huge trees. The sliding glass door in her living room provided a view to the world outside. The bathroom was equipped with all of the necessary grab bars and could accommodate her wheelchair and walker. With her approval, we moved her during the first week in December.

Although she wasn't declining rapidly, both of Mom's doctors advised us to enroll her into Hospice, and we did. Things calmed down for awhile as my mother settled into her new living arrangement. She socialized a bit and looked forward to visits from the family, most days having at least 2 or 3 of us spending time with her. She was still reluctant to have staff assist and help her.

Before we knew it, it was February. Then, the day after Valentine's Day Mom fell again. She had not wanted to call for help from the staff. Her legs buckled as she was getting out of bed. One of my sisters was there. Unable to get my mother off of the floor, she called for help from the staff. An ambulance took her to emergency.

Although she didn't break anything, that fall was the turning point. She had been jarred once too many times, and was quickly declining on so many levels.

I helped as much as I could. Most times, I just couldn't get it right. It was hard to get her comfortable physically and to calm her emotionally. She was angry, she was scared. She said she didn't believe in God, yet asked why God was punishing her.

I suggested a visit from a Prayer Chaplain. She agreed and I arranged for someone I knew to come. It was a good fit. She would say to him, "You're quite a guy," and he would reply, "You're quite a gal." He'd bless her with the Prayer for Protection. She had heard me say it before. It was her favorite prayer. I wrote it out so that it could be read to her by whoever was there, should she ask for it.

Then one day while I was visiting Mom she insisted on getting out of bed and wanted me to help. I called the staff from her apartment and begged her to wait until they came. She refused and started sitting up, sliding her legs over the bed and trying to stand. She wouldn't stop trying to get up, pushing me, and yelling, "Why won't you help me? Why won't you help me?" Through tears, I cried, "I don't want you to fall Mom. I love you."

Finally, they came, and helped Mom out of bed. I kissed her goodbye and left. I was still crying as I drove home. I thought of how scared I was when she was trying to get up, how desperately I didn't want her to fall, and how *helpless* I felt. Just like I felt when I was 8 years old after daddy died. Helpless! I began to sob and had to pull over and stop the car. Finally, I had calmed down, and turned the ignition on.

As I drove home a haiku popped into my head. In perfect rhythm and meter:

feeling so helpless
and the answer is simple
help less, yes, help less

I called my brother as soon as I got home and asked, "Do you remember hearing Mom wailing and crying to records after Daddy died?"

"No," he said, "I was outside digging for worms."

The next six weeks were filled with a lot of love rather than fear. I helped less and realized that I had no control over my mother falling or not. It was not in my power to help keep my mother from falling now or when I was a little girl.

No matter how hard I tried or how badly I wanted it, it wasn't mine to do. There were also other areas where my "helping" Mom was me wanting things to go a certain way. I had been stepping up and inserting myself even when she hadn't asked me to. I let go.

On March 27, 2014 my sisters called and said I should probably come over to Mom's. She wasn't doing well. When I got there Mom was sitting in her wheelchair at a table leaning forward. My sisters sat on either side of her holding her hands. I kissed the side of Mom's face and stood behind her, leaning over her, as close as I could get, I wrapped my arms around her.

I said, "I've got you Mom, I've got you," and then blessed her with the Prayer for Protection:

The Light of God surrounds you
The Love of God enfolds you
The power of God protects you
The presence of God watches over you
Wherever you are, God is!

– *James Dillet Freeman*

She then settled in under a comfy blanket in her reclining chair. She said she heard her father calling her. He was saying, "Come."

On March 28, 2014, just before dawn she let go of this earth. Guided by the Light, she left our arms and went into the arms of her father.

Chapter Three

EXPECTING TIME TO ALLOW US TO MAKE ADJUSTMENTS

OTHERWISE KNOWN AS:

If I Had Only Known

I remembered her liberating me, and I hoped I would be
able to liberate her; she deserved that from me...

— Maya Angelou

As we have learned from Keebler-Ross and others, there are stages of grief and loss which are not necessarily linear. Rather, they overlap, sometimes coming back to haunt us again and again. Memories come upon us from out of nowhere – especially if we think we have healed or transformed them already. We may need to uncurl our fists and surrender to the emotions one more time, as we allow ourselves to let go of our mothers.

There are other thoughts we may need to also let go of, if we cannot accept and embrace them...that we are not like our mothers – we did not bring any of her ways of doing and being into our own lives and our own homes – that we are our own person, completely separate from anything from our past.

And then, again, we may be able to relax and see the beautiful connection that was maintained, if not nurtured and cultivated even as we thought we were separating our lives from hers.

Looking at this tiny person who loomed so much larger in your life, you hesitate to say the word "goodbye." Instead you feel the rush of love words bumping up against that lump in your throat, you sort through them for the proper ones, the ones that will show her the respect, but will allow you to keep your own.

I love you, Mama – Everything will be fine. We are OK, now.

...We both can let go.

The Crucifix

Elizabeth French

©2006

Uh oh, "Sorry, Mom," I muttered to myself, feeling the smooth surface of the crucifix brush my hand as it swung from my rearview mirror. "I know I took that corner too fast. I'll try to remember to slow down next time." Mom still watches over me and tries to keep me from endangering myself. I know she is there, because she always has tried to protect me, and because she sends me a message every time the crucifix touches my skin.

I had made a deal with my Dad to meet me half way from my house and his... in Solvang, California. It was June, 2005, nearly a year to the date my Mother had died. He was eighty-seven years young – still powerful and healthy. I figured it would be good for him to get away from the home he had shared with my Mother for almost sixty-three years of marriage. Actually, it was 62 years 8 months and 28 days together, to be precise. I really didn't want him to be alone. After such a long and loving marriage, he felt very sad and lost without the love of his life: the woman he was totally committed to.

"There is a casino in Santa Inez," I said to him. "Get yourself up and drive on over to meet me." He made the four hour drive and met me at Anderson's Split Pea Soup Restaurant. After finding our room in a pleasant, Danish-looking motel, we went to the casino and had fun gambling the first night. The next morning as we talked, we decided it would be special to go to the Solvang Mission – to light a candle, say some prayers and take some moments to think of Mom. And hug and hold her near and dear to our hearts.

We arrived at the mission only to find a chapel full of people celebrating a wedding. We stepped inside and found there was no way we were going to light a candle or find a quiet peaceful moment to reflect on Mom. What to do?

"Dad, let's walk around the grounds and find a spot to sit and think of Mom." As we walked around the outer hallways we saw a plaque on the wall. It announced the day the mission was commissioned: the date was the same date my Mother had died, January 28th. My Dad touched it and cried. I did too. But I wanted to be strong and help him through it. Wow. Here we were, at the very same date – a time too precious for us to deal with at this point – both trying to get away from the sadness and yet seeing it clearly in almost everything we did.

We continued our walk through the grounds, hoping the wedding guests would soon disperse so we could complete our mission (no pun intended). As we walked around I kept opening doors hoping to find a small chapel. We found a room set with candelabras in sets of eight or ten, all lit; but no extra candles anywhere. Being curious and wanting to light a candle, I began to open closet door after closet door. Still no candles to light, Dang it. In one closet I found a plastic crucifix. I put it in my pocket.

Finally we were able to find a spot of quiet. We prayed, said some nice things about Mother and started to leave the mission. The wedding was still going on. Dad wished the couple a long and happy life together.

October 2001

Dad always took care of Mom and kept her confusion a secret from my brother and me. I guess he didn't want us to worry. We'd talk on the phone and they would both get on an extension, like they had always done. He'd say, "Frances, say 'Hi!'." She would. He'd say, "Didn't we have a great day?"

And she'd say, "Yes, we had a great day. And who am I talking to?" He was good. She followed his lead. I didn't really know that Mom had gotten to a stage of really not having a clue. Mom seemed happy, but only on his lead.

Then my brother and I visited Mom and Dad in October 2001 for his birthday. It was horrible. She would walk out of the living room and then return and say, "Hi, nice to see you." My brother kidded that Mom was always glad to see us each time she walked back into the room. Dad couldn't leave her alone for a minute. I was totally freaked out. I couldn't believe she really didn't know who we were or what was going on.

I'd say, "Mom, I'm your daughter." She actually talked about the person who was her daughter to me. I guess she was happy with the person, or me, that in her mind was her daughter. She'd tell me about things that her daughter was doing. I was her daughter and she did not know me. It hurt! Selfishly I wanted her to know me… the daughter that loved her.

I'd say, "Mom, I'm your girl." She still didn't know me. She was projecting a lot of hate in her life then. She didn't like what was happening to her.

Mom could still play a great game of "Kings in the Corner." What's with that? She would talk to her Dad in Nantucket; "Daddy, I'll go to the store and get some bread if you give me five cents."

I stayed longer than my brother and continued to play games and tried to figure out what the heck was going on… reality was getting too real. Mom thought I was Dad's girlfriend and was fighting me for each moment of his time, which he generously gave her because he was always watching out for her. Mom didn't want me in the house because she thought I was trying to take her boyfriend away from her.

There were times when Mom would try to get outside to watch the house next door because the Secret Service had told her that the President was coming to visit the neighbor's house. She'd stand there and watch for a long time. I'd stand beside her and she would tell me how she was contacted by those special people and couldn't let anything happen to that house that would endanger the President. I could only relate this to her childhood when she lived on the Cape and the Kennedy's lived nearby. I don't know. But she was serious about the burden of watching that house.

January 2002

Dad called me and said Mom had pneumonia and was in the Hemet hospital. The doctors wanted to send her to an Extended Care facility for a few days to make sure all was well. I now believe it was also because the doctor realized Dad needed some time away from the constant care giving responsibilities.

I drove down; and Dad and I visited Mom in the Extended Care facility. It was crazy. I guess there are too many people in those places. The nurses were over burdened and appeared to be hardened to their plights.

In this place they put my Mother in a room and strapped her down. When she wasn't strapped down, they put her in a wheel chair with a pillow that kept her from moving in a natural way. She couldn't get anywhere outside the wheel chair. She could scoot around with her legs, which caused her to lose her shoes and socks, and they'd get mad and tie her down. She really didn't like that. She'd grab at her legs and belly and say, "I hate what's happening to me." So, was she aware? Yes, I believe she was. She didn't like not knowing what was going on in her life. She hated not being the Frances French that she'd always been. Even in her delusion she knew that something was wrong. She also knew that she loved a man named Milton.

This Extended Care place decided that they were in control of her life at that point. They cut her beautiful hair. It had always been kept short and well cared for Peggy, a good friend and caring person. But they shaved her head so that it wouldn't be a problem for "them" at the facility. I did not recognize my Mother when I walked into the place. She was in a wheelchair stuffed with a pillow so she couldn't move, and her hair was close cut. And they had lost her upper denture teeth. From then on she could never actually eat solid food. She had little or no reason to live. All she ever wanted was my Dad. All he ever wanted was my Mom.

Today

I still have the crucifix hanging on my rearview mirror. When I turn a corner in my car and it swings and touches my hand, I know it's my Mother sending me a message; sending me her love. When I hit the brakes for a red light and it swings back and forth and touches my hand again and I reach out and touch it's smooth surface, the plastic cross feels good in my hand and I say, "Thanks Mom, you are right, I should slow down, I should think about that before I make a decision. I'd hate to go over the side of this curvy road without giving my thoughts and love to those I love, while I'm still driving this road and still have my mind so that my precious son, Thomas, doesn't have to feel any pain."

Oh, and by the way, I'm not Catholic.

DIFFICULT DIVA MOM

Jerrine Minkus Rowley

©2006

If I said that my mother was a difficult woman, everyone who knew her would reel back in shock and shriek, "Difficult? That doesn't even come close! Diva would be more like it."

Of course, my mother never thought of herself as a diva. More, she would have been quite offended that anyone could have thought her difficult. That's how unaware she was – how totally out of touch with her own emotions or those of her loved ones.

Possibly most daughters think of their mothers as difficult, at one time or another in their lives. It's just that, there was never a time that I didn't find my mother difficult. As a child, a teenager, a young adult, and even up until the day she died in 1999, at the age of 81 – My mother was difficult.

She was the sort of woman that, on Mothers' Day, I could never buy a typical flowery Mothers' Day Card, full of love and appreciation.

I think she would have liked a flowery loving card, but I couldn't bring myself to do it. It would have been too much of a lie. So I usually got a blank card and wrote something nice in it – as nice as I could anyway. In truth, she actually asked me once why I never got her a flowery card, and I said that I just don't like those kinds of cards, and don't buy anyone cards like that. I felt I had to lie.

I always imagined when I got older that her anger was caused from layer upon layer of hurt that she would never talk about it. She didn't have much personal insight, about herself or others, so it would have been nearly impossible for her to talk about herself.

She was critical and judgmental about almost everything. I could hardly do anything right by her. It wasn't only directed at me, she was also very negative about my father. My brother had it easier, because, as in many Jewish families, the boy is "prince." But she was negative about most people, whether in or out of our immediate family, showing little compassion or understanding of anyone different from her – which most people were, of course.

My mother was all business, and not much heart. I think she cared very deeply, and she actually did a lot for people, so she didn't quite understand why people didn't respond to her as she thought they should. She was actually very confusing in that way. On the materialistic level, she did a lot for me when I was growing up – taking me places to be with friends, buying me things. I could always count on her. I really appreciated that about her. She always kept a good home, always cooked good meals, did everything a mother was supposed to do, but when it came to emotions, she just never could understand them. I needed a mother who was loving and emotionally supportive, and I never got that from her. I never heard "I love you" in words. Purchases and deeds simply never made up for that.

I remember one time at camp. I was probably nine or ten. One night I was crying so hard in my bunk, that the counselor came over to comfort me.

"Jerrine, honey, what's the matter? Tell me about it and maybe we can work things out together."

"I can't. I can't," I cried, having nothing to do with that! I thought, 'Why is she being so nice to me? What is she after? Who is she going to tell? I'm going to get into real trouble if I tell her anything.' I simply had no experience with anyone being so nice to me and wanting to help me through a difficult time.

What had happened at camp was what many young girls go through at that age, but I had no idea I could reach out for help from any adult. I wanted to tell her, "My friends were mean to me because I made friends with Susan, and they don't like Susan ," but it was as if I had been paralyzed and couldn't speak.

Rejected by my friends, unable to reach out for help, I was sure I would go through life feeling just like I did at that moment. Hurt. Sad. Unloved. I decided to reach out to my mother.

I called her on the phone. "Mom, something terrible happened." Silence met my ears.

"I can't wait to come home, Mom." Silence again.

"Mom?"

"Yes?"

"I'll tell you about it when you pick me up on Saturday."

"Fine. Is that all?"

"I guess."

"Well, don't be such a big baby. You're supposed to be having fun. I'll see you on Saturday."

Saturday didn't come soon enough. When the Mercedes pulled up, I hopped in and it all came out at once. "They just don't like me. I made friends with Susan and they were just so mean, and they don't like Susan and I wanted them to like me and Susan, too and why do they have to be so mean, Mom? I just don't understand it. Why did they do that to me?"

My mother's eyes never left the center of the roadway as we drove away. My mother's head never moved from side to side in confirmation or condemnation of those girls. My mother's lips never parted to even to begin to utter even one single word of recognition, understanding or comfort.

I realized then and there that she just couldn't understand. "Why do I keep trying?" I thought. "She does this every time." That same reaction of silence and utter non-involvement had happened so many times prior to that day, all I could do was sink deeper into the seat, stare straight ahead and feel rejected again – by my own mother.

As the years came and went, I became immured to the silence and the unopened heart, and I suppose I came to believe that this was the way all families lived. But I always held out the hope that love existed, somewhere, somehow.

"Do you love daddy?" I asked her often as a child. Never having seen affection or warmth or even friendship, I knew that these were expressions I had seen from other parents I knew. Of course, I was too young to understand why I asked that question.

"Why do you ask?" was her standard reply.

I remember years later, in my teens, asking her, "How did you know daddy was the one?"

"I knew he'd provide a good living."

Made sense, I guess. We lived well. We always had everything we wanted. I never lacked for anything.

One time when I was a senior in high school and went out to lunch, she asked me, "Was I good mother?"

What could I say that wouldn't hurt her feelings? "Yeah, sure" was my meek reply.

"Well, if I had to do it over again, I wouldn't have had kids."

I sat there speechless. This was definitely too much information, for a change, and certainly not the kind of information she should be sharing with her daughter.

If only she had said, "You know, I always wanted to be a doctor, and I didn't do it, and I wish I had," it might have filled the silence with something positive. It might have led me to understand her better. It may have become clear that it wasn't having me that depressed her, but it was never achieving something she had always wanted to achieve. But no. It was me.

Home for a visit from college one weekend a year later, I found the courage to say, "I never felt loved by you."

Mom's response was most shocking: "How could you say that? I gave you everything you could ever want!"

I realize now Mom thought that was showing her love – giving me things, buying me things. She thought that should be enough. I was speechless. How could I explain to my own mother that that isn't love. I didn't need things from her. That is not to say that I didn't appreciate the things. Much to the contrary. I loved having new clothes and a car to drive. But I wasn't in the position, or didn't want to take the position, of having to explain to my mother that I needed more from her. She should have known. Any loving mother would have known. Any loving mother would have been happy to see me happy.

Some people, you just can't make happy. She would have been happy had I married a rich, Jewish man. I think, from what she said to me when I was younger, before I married the first time, that was all she cared about. Whether he was really a good person, whether we had a fantastic relationship or a real friendship, this didn't seem to matter to her. She cared more about "show" than the things that really mattered to me. She thought about how proud she could be to her friends if I married some successful Jewish guy, not whether or not I was happy. Since I never was attracted to the type of man she wanted me to marry, my marriages never made her happy. But I have to wonder about her happiness. She did marry a good provider, but happiness was never a part of that picture.

I know my dad had had affairs while I was growing up, but I never knew if my mom knew about them. Maybe she did. Maybe that is what made her so unhappy and angry. Maybe that's why she always was annoyed at him. Of course, on the other hand, maybe he had affairs because, as I saw it, she was always angry and annoyed at him.

When I fell in love, I was determined to not be like my mother. I met my first husband in college and actually, I understood later, that he was really a lot like my mother. Controlling and critical of me, it continued a pattern I was very familiar with by that time. My mother, of course, didn't like Larry at all, and when I finally told her I was going to end it, she wouldn't let me live it down.

"Of course I'm not going to tell you 'I told you so'. Just look for someone like your father next time."

Trying my very best to not look for my father next time, my second husband was a good friend first. He was a nice enough guy, but we should have stayed just friends. My mom liked him. Dad loved him, but I found he was way too much like my dad; passive, non-communicative, and also very critical. We divorced.

"My God, Jerrine! All you ever do is embarrass me. Another divorce? Can't you stick with anything? What are people going to say?"

Marriage didn't feel like any kind of institution for me for many years after that, but when I met David, everything just fell into place. My past was my past. Lessons learned were good ones, and finally, David is the most wonderful person I know and our marriage is nothing like the ones I had always known.

My father appreciated David. He valued people for who they were more than my mom ever could. Mom just couldn't like him. She was always "polite", sending him birthday cards on his birthday, including him on our family trips, etc. But she never "got him" and I knew that, probably because David values communication, emotional depth, and acceptance rather than criticism.

For those same reasons, my mother was never able to "get me" either. So much unlike her, I never placed a value on the same things, although we did like a lot of the same things, superficially and materially. We both enjoyed cats, football, going out to eat, movies. We liked to travel. We would share books and we would talk occasionally on the phone. Sometimes these conversations would go well and I liked her. But more times than not, she would pick up the phone, saying "Hello" in that critical edgy tone of hers, like you knew you just interrupted her from her favorite TV show. And when we were together, it always sounded like the same old records of the same old criticisms about everything I did – everything I liked – everything I was. Her criticism of me was dominant.

In later years, my dad started saying things that hurt me and, when I chose to voice my opinions and stand up for myself, my mom would say, "How could you feel that way? He loves you more than anyone."

One time, when we were all together at a party, my dad was asked, "Did you guys ever think about having any more children than Jerrine and her older brother?"

"No, the first one was a surprise and the second was a disappointment, so we stopped there."

That cut deep, of course. "That hurts my feelings, Dad."

"Oh, grow up," she replied for him. "You're always trying to find something wrong with us. You don't understand anything."

My perceptions are always wrong. That's just the way it is. That's the message I always got from them whenever I reacted emotionally or tried to communicate about my feelings.

I know I disappointed my parents. Possibly because I was too honest. My mother never liked that at all. She never understood that it was important to me to be loved for who I truly am, even if it meant confession of a difficult truth. My mother didn't take well to the truth.

When I had an abortion before my first husband and I decided to get married, my mother was only embarrassed and disappointed. Comfort, support, and concern were simply not in her makeup. I came from an average family, not highly educated, nor especially talented. So the expectations weren't particularly high. No matter what I ever did or did not do, I always felt disappointment from them both – never pride, satisfaction, nor support. Only cold disappointment – scornful embarrassment.

Even as an adult, when I would call up, "Hi Mom, I'm going to come down and visit."

"I'm looking forward to seeing you," she would say.

I would come into the house. There she would be, standing stiff if I went up to give her a hug, arms by her side, unable to respond with any kind of motherly warmth. She did this so often, that saying hello or goodbye was always a painful experience.

Sometimes I see that I have become like my mother in ways I never thought I would. I go out of my way to do things for others. Then I feel hurt and angry if they don't respond to me the way I think they should. And I wonder sometimes, 'Do people see me like they did her?'

Where is the girl who was more free and open? I take care of business rather well. I am reliable and dependable just like her. I do my chores. I have my warm and affectionate side, however, it is hard to let go. It is hard to relax, but unlike my mother, I am able to step back and look at myself with some insight and resolve to grow.

While some lack of confidence is still there, I am, unlike my mother, quite introspective. When she felt the same insecurity she simply covered it up with "why can't everyone be like me?" And she seriously meant it! I, on the other hand, feel the insecurity but am able to question myself, especially doubting my emotional reaction to things. Is this appropriate? Is it OK that I feel this? Their criticisms of me are continued sometimes by my own inner voice.

What Dad said, "the second was a disappointment" must have been true for them, and it left its mark on me. I still don't take criticism very well. And on the flip side of the coin, I myself can be sometimes more critical than I should be of others.

Not wanting to live my life as a victim, I try to be vigilant and aware of my mother's influences on me, and that helps me to understand my own reactions. But it doesn't stop me from feeling short-changed. I needed a loving mother. I deserved a mother who would be on my side and support me even if I was wrong. I wanted to be able to give flowery Mothers' Day cards on Mothers' Day.

So my biggest goal in life has been to be in a loving successful relationship and thankfully, I have succeeded in my marriage with David. I met David when I was 43 and he 39, and we've been together now for 26 years. Even though I didn't have the role models I needed. Even though I had many "false starts" in prior relationships, I do not regret any of my experiences. Here I am. Happy. Healthy. And in a loving relationship.

And when I think of my mom now, I am grateful I don't have any regrets in terms of "If I had only…" I was aware that I didn't want to reach the end of her life feeling that way, so I always attempted to have a good relationship with her and be honest. I did everything I knew how to do, in order to connect with her. Never mind that most of the time it just never quite worked. I don't blame myself.

More than a difficult woman, my mother was a diva, and I know I am not. And by the way, I get lots of flowery cards full of love and appreciation from my husband, David. Even if it's not Mothers' Day.

SAYING SOLLY

Nora J. Stone

©2006

My mother is Japanese, born in Nagoya, Japan, 1931, and was a War Bride. My Father looked like Willie Nelson: White as he wanted to be, red hair with freckles, and was living in a trailer outside of Jackson, Mississippi when he died. We're the original Rice Crackers. I'm like a Nissan Truck: conceived in Japan but manufactured locally.

Mom met Dad during the Occupation. She danced at the USO for hamburgers that she'd sneak to my uncles through the fence. She felt "to the victors go the spoils," and she was the best Japan had to offer America, so she came here on a boat, the same boat as Helen Keller. Mom thought the brass band at the dock was for the War Brides. Instead all the War Brides' paperwork was messed up and all of them landed in jail until it could be straightened out. Mom met oatmeal for the first time in jail, pregnant with me, my older sister Linda still a babe in her arms. I don't think Mom likes oatmeal for breakfast to this day.

When Mom is drunk she does a wicked imitation of Helen Keller addressing the officials. She couldn't see or hear, but they nevertheless met her when the boat docked. "Why have a band for Helen Keller? She can't hear it, it's stupid," Mom said when she'd finish the merciless imitation. I can see her stabbing out a cigarette, still angry at her reception to America.

Dad disappeared somewhere along the way when I was a little baby and it took me until I was 35 years old to find him. Mom didn't speak to me for a couple of years afterward, for she had issues about my search for my Dad. She tends to take things personally instead of seriously, but that's Mom.

It was hard for my Mom, being a single mother, having a couple of bad marriages, and having three daughters whose birth gave her no honor. "If I had known I'd have given birth to three weird bitches like you, I'd have jumped off the bridge before my first period," she often said in frustration. "We love you too, Mom," we'd reply laughing, but her words still stung.

Sorry is a big deal in a family that's half-Japanese. There's this joke we have in the family that being Japanese means always having to say you're sorry. You're sorry for being fat, stupid and ugly. You're sorry for not being on honor roll. You're sorry that you weren't born a boy. You're definitely sorry to be half-Japanese when being anything else would have been much easier.

Throughout my whole life I never remembered my mother ever saying she was sorry, except once. When she did we were traumatized. Linda, Mom and I were talking around my sister's kitchen table late one night. Holidays were always spent at my sister's home in the suburbs because it was a bigger place than Mom's and much better than any place I had. So after cleaning up after dinner in a way that a Virgo sister would approve of, we're sitting there having tea and munching on Japanese tea crackers; "Eating for entertainment," as Mom would say.

The kids were asleep up stairs. Five out of seven grandsons were there. Mom once said, "If I lived in Japan I'd be given a medal for all these grandsons." I thought to myself, "Yeah, as they stuffed our sons head first into the mouths of cannons to shoot at unsuspecting neighbors, no thank you." My brother-in-law was hiding upstairs pretending to sleep, just to avoid us.

Mom had this look on her face, a "bikuri" face; scary, like she was about to choke on a cracker.

"What's the matter?" I asked her, ready to do the Heimlich maneuver.

She sighs, long and slow, pushing around some tea crackers with her long painted nails.

"I have to say sorry," she says with this pained expression.

"To whom?" I ask. I'm the English Major. I can say "whom" when I wish. Linda shoots me a look as if to say, "Show off."

"To you two girls," Mom says. No matter how old we get we're still "girls" and we're always the "two girls." No individuality here, individuality is equal to insanity to Mom. That's why I'm always in hot water with her.

It's really getting bikuri now. Mom never says "sorry" unless it's for something small like bumping into you in a crowded kitchen, not for serious stuff, which has always been an issue for me.

"Mom! What's the Matter?" Linda says, half getting up out of her chair. I thought she was going to go over and feel Mom's forehead to see if there was any sign of fever.

Mom started to cry. Now that's just the limit. Mom doesn't cry at the drop of a hat like I do. Not like Linda when she's watching sad movies. Now we fear she has cancer or something awful and she didn't tell us in time, and now it's too late.

"I'm sorry...," Mom starts, wiping her eyes with a dish towel, "that I was such a coward when you two were young."

Now, where does all this come from? Linda was 33 and I was 32 years old. What sort of sad memory from our childhood is she going to dredge up? That she left our Father for no good purpose? That she picked a horrible Step Father for a second husband? That she was a cocktail waitress for 32 years and we had to run the home and care for our little sister at night? That nothing we do is ever good enough? What on earth is she going to say "solly" for?

Truth be known, all that Mom had to go through, Linda and I felt took a lot of courage: Leaving Japan when she was a teen-ager; Coming to America and not knowing the language; Ending up in Mississippi where she discovered she was a "colored gal and a Jap;" Striking out on her own with two babies; Being the first Japanese woman to be hired at "The Showboat" bar and restaurant; Being the first War Bride in her group of girlfriends to own or drive a car, to own a home, to retire early. Where did she lack courage?

Linda gets up and goes over to hug Mom, and Mom shies away. Physical contact with a Japanese parent is a highly choreographed affair. Don't hug the shoulder. Touch the forearm, that's enough.

"Mom, when were you ever a coward?" Linda tries to give comfort and is rebuffed with a wave of a dishtowel.

"Mom, you were very brave. You went through a lot that was difficult," I protest, but don't try to give her physical comfort. I took "Intercultural Communication between Americans and the Japanese" in College. I know better.

Linda gives up and sits down again. Doing the "Enryo-shimasu," giving Mom space out of deference. I decide to wait until Mom dredges up what ever is giving her that look on her face. We "girls" sit and wait with tight stomachs and pursed lips.

"I want to say 'sorry' for not being brave enough to kill you and your sister and kill myself. Instead I was a coward and the two of you

83

had shitty lives," Mom blurts out, looking at my sister, and starts woo hooing in the dishtowel.

Linda jumps like she's been bitten by a snake. I have to slap my mouth with my hand and hold it there hard, because I'm about to call my mother crazy. Linda and I look at one another in that secret sister eyeball language that says, "What's going on? I don't know. Is she crazy? Go figure. What should we do? You're asking me?" all in a glance and a few eyebrow moves.

"Mom, is this some Japanese thing we're not understanding completely?" I ask, keeping emotional distance and hiding behind intellect. Mom's a mess and doesn't seem to hear me. I turn to my sister and whisper, "You got to believe in reincarnation to have these feelings and get away with it." Linda nods in agreement with eyes big as saucers.

"Mom, I'm sure that Nora and I are very grateful that you weren't brave enough to kill us and commit suicide," Linda says slowly, trying to sound sane while stringing those words together. I can imagine how Linda must feel having her life be called "shitty." Linda's been the perfect older daughter, did all that was expected of her, stayed with Mom until Mom's home was paid off, paying half of everything. Linda got a job and kept it, got a working husband and owns a home and rental property, only birthed boys. Where is her life supposed to be so awful? Linda takes things personally too.

This is getting just too surreal and I'm starting to split my personality just to deal with it. I look out the kitchen sliding glass doors. Linda's back yard is butt-up against a cemetery. Bad Feng Shui probably had an effect on that marriage. The light from the kitchen only illuminated the back porch, but you knew the graves were a stone's throw away in the dark. The darkness was as impenetrable as my mother's despair.

I thought to myself of all the times Mom could have done us in.

When Mom walked us along Lake Merritt in Oakland to feed the ducks. When she took us to the beach. When she walked with us along cliffs in Big Sur. When she drove about with us bouncing around in the back seat of that Impala convertible, in the days before seat belts and child safety seats. All the times she said it was OK to ride in the back of the pick up truck of my Step Father. Suddenly a free childhood looked like a reckless childhood, with my mother hoping we'd buy the farm in some accident.

Was she thinking all those times, "Should I kill my daughters here?" Then stopping herself not out of concern for our lives, but because she was a coward, then hating herself for lacking the guts to go through with it. Does Mom still feel that way? Is that what Mom's been writing in her diary in Japanese all these years? Did Linda and I have such faulty psychic ability never to have felt her dark thoughts?

Now I know I'm an American. It would never occur to me to kill my children because I went through some patch of hard times. I don't have such a low threshold of embarrassment. I would never think of killing myself because things didn't turn out as I had so ardently hoped. This is the land of opportunity and things can always get better. I would feel successful if I did have suicidal thoughts and got over it.

Mom's still weeping, neither of us "girls" making any effort to comfort her. We don't feel like comforting her. I feel like giving her a smack. I'm reeling with the implications of her confession.

Linda's in shock, probably running through all the possible times when she and I were happily skipping along the beach, hand in hand, oblivious to our Mother's murder/suicide thoughts. If Linda gives it too much thought she's likely to get angry and start a fight. There've been more than one evening that Linda and Mom's fights have spilled out into the softly scented Fremont nights, entertaining the neighbors on the cul-de-sac. "There they go again, " is what I figured the neighbors said to each other when they watched.

It's not just our lives we were reviewing. We have 5 out of 7 grandsons of this crazy woman, upstairs sleeping innocently. None of them would have been born had she been brave enough to kill us when we were little girls. I know my maternal protective urges were kicked up a notch at that moment of realization.

I've got to do something to stem the tide of this escalating into a family brawl caused by the three of us falling into a gap in intercultural communication.

"Mom, you don't need to say sorry," I tell her. "We happen to like our shitty lives." I couldn't help but start laughing. "No matter what happens, we only have to look to you to find our courage and keep on trying. So even though you were feeling like a coward we only saw you as being brave." I was proud of myself for coming up with that roundabout way of letting her off the hook and still saying what I needed to say. Linda is nodding enthusiastically in agreement, looking relieved at my making an effort to stop this conversation.

"Really?" Mom says, sniffling. "Leely?" her accent echoes in my head.

Yeah, really. Since she never admitted to her lack of courage when we were little, we only knew what we saw. All we saw was a woman who didn't take a lot of guff. We saw a woman who left her country and came to a land where she had lost all her previous status. We saw someone learn how to cook, when we knew she had a maid throughout the entire war to stand in food ration lines for her. We saw a woman who learned how to sew because buying off the rack clothing was too expensive. We had her teach us how to cook, sew, knit and crochet, so we'd be useful. More useful than she was when she got here. We had her teach us origami, ink brush painting and art appreciation so we'd be more than just useful. She had to learn a whole new language and that showed us that there was more than one way to look at life. She did everything she could to support us. We saw her become American when we were raised that way through cultural osmosis.

So as much as I still have "issues to address" with my Mother, I realize it's because she's Japanese who had to become American, and it took a toll on her. I'm an American who has a Mother who expects me to automatically understand what being Japanese is all about, and I have to take College classes to understand her.

This was one situation where I won't accept Mom's apology. I like my life no matter how much it doesn't live up to her expectations. I did share this story with my four sons and they all thanked me for living long enough to birth them, because they like their lives too.

ANOTHER COMPANION FOR SAINT DONNA

Billie Ruth Hopkins Furuichi

©2006

Four dogs and a cat are already with Mom, I like to believe: I like to picture Blondie, Buddy, Baron, Duke, and Fuzzy as her spiritual companions for almost two years now. Blondie was our family dog growing up. She was one of those huge mongrels who let us ride her like a horse. Mom always knew when we were coming home from school, because Blondie would get up, scratch on the door to be let out, amble to the corner of Ogden and Louisiana everyday at 3 pm, sit and wait for us. Mom always said she was the smartest of all our dogs.

Buddy was next and he was smart, too. One August, getting back from Mexico, we were busily unpacking, and suddenly Mom says, "Where's Buddy?" We searched up and down the block for him, but he was nowhere in sight. Then the telephone rang.

"Welcome Home!" It was Gran, who lived almost five miles south on Downing Street.

"How did you know we were back?" Mom asked.

"Well, Buddy just came up to the door and told me."

Mom and Dad got Duke from a neighbor when they lived in Indian Hills. Then, Baron just showed up one day and decided he liked it there.

"Baron was so dumb, and so sweet," Mom always said. After Dad died, Baron would come to her on the couch, and whine. He would push her hand up with his nose and plead with her to get up and go outside with him. He wasn't so dumb after all, making sure Mom got fresh air and exercise when she actually had no intention of going on at all.

Fuzzy, the cat, lived to be at least eighteen, spending her retirement years in the Indian Hills cabin where my Pioneer Woman Mom lived without electricity or running water while Dad finished the big house fifty yards uphill. I remember stopping in from California when I was about thirty-two, so Mom had to be about fifty-seven. I was on my way to field trial a technical training package we had just finished for Wisconsin Telephone, and Mom had baked bread in the iron wood stove. I remember being in awe that she not only endured this lifestyle for nearly three years before moving into a real house, but that she even seemed to like it.

It was no surprise, really.

"I'll live anywhere with your Pop," she would always say. And she meant it. He was her only love. Her life, her breath, her reason for living, no matter the circumstances. The day she spotted him from across the Golden High School swimming pool when she was fourteen, she said to herself, "There's my man." Poor Bill, never had a chance, even though Grampa Owen truly disliked him for at least twenty years.

"Ya' marry a jack ass, you'll breed jack asses," he scolded, but Grampa's opinion didn't count for much by then. By the age of nineteen, Mom knew exactly what she wanted, and she figured she knew exactly how to get it, too. As Dad was going off to the Army, they got engaged, and he asked his best friend, Bob, to take care of Donna.

"Sure," Bob agreed gleefully, then proceeded to court her big time.

Bill got wind of all this, came back on Leave, confronted Donna. She nodded matter-of-factly, "Yeah, Bob is sure a swell guy. You know, he wants to marry me! What do you think we should do, Bill?"

They were married during that very Leave.

Both sets of parents at first refused to attend the wedding, but Gran Owen ended up relenting. After all, Donna was her oldest daughter and she had to be there since Grampa wasn't going to give her away. The only one on the Hopkins side who came was Uncle Dick. He and Dad were considered the black sheep Democrats, what with Grandmother Hopkins being DAR and all. I remember always feeling as if I had to sit up really straight whenever we were in her presence, which was rare enough. Grandmother Hopkins attended neither their wedding nor much of the rest of their lives, as I recall.

Mom and Dad were a startlingly attractive couple. I grew up thinking Mom looked like Jennifer Jones and Dad could have been Edward G. Robinson, only more slender in the face. I idolized them both and couldn't hear their story of rebellion enough, forcing them to tell it over and over again. They were deeply in love and my father was always the one in charge, so there was never a doubt in my mind that being a good wife came with acquiescence and sacrifice. If Pop didn't like avocados, well then, avocados simply did not exist. If Dad couldn't stand the smell of shrimp, by golly, the creepy creatures wouldn't dare set foot in our refrigerator. But I remember every December twentieth when we went out to dinner for Mom's birthday, Mom ordered deep fried shrimp and avocado salad. Every year.

All three of us kids grew up scorning football. It wasn't until years after my father's death when Mom had finally remarried, that I was the shocked witness one Sunday afternoon, to my mother, perched on the edge of her couch in front of the TV set, yelling at the Bronco's coach, "Over the top! Over the top!" Without a clue as to what she was so excited about, I watched in amazement. The Broncos were lined up right on the goal line then somehow one of them was doing a flying forward roll over the other team.

My sixty-five year old Mom stands up, both arms extended high over her head, "Go Broncos!" Then she does this little two-step dance in a circle while punching the air, sits down, takes a sip of beer and hisses between her teeth, "Boy, it's a good thing he listens to me, huh?"

My jaw was probably almost to my chest. "Mom?"

"Sure, Doll, I was in the high school band, remember? I always did love football – it was your Pop who couldn't stand it."

At that moment, I saw a woman who I wanted to get to know a whole lot better. The Mom I had known all my life never put her needs first, worried far too much about her children, always found a way, on Dad's meager teacher's salary, to give us what we needed, had fun giving us birthday parties and singing with us in the Greater Denver Opera Association; drove every kid in the neighborhood to every function imaginable, smiled and cheered at our every dance, violin and piano recital; but never, never did I see my mother get excited about anything in life, like she was that Sunday over the Broncos going over the top for a touchdown.

While we were growing up, taking care of us was how she took her life over the top – that, of course, and a tendency for excessive worry. She worried if she didn't have anything to worry about, and while she had every reason to worry, she took it to extremes. And why not! Frought with mishap, pain and disappointment from the day of that marriage, her life was a trial of Biblical proportions, yet she endured, she overcame, she survived, she flourished. Strong, pure and unconditionally loving, my Saint Donna was a powerful woman who sometimes had to go after life like she was killing snakes. Grampa Owen told her that when my sister, Bobbie, was burned at the age of three. "Sometimes, Donna, you just have to go after life like you was killin' snakes," he said. And that's pretty much how she lived right up until the end.

A lesser woman would have buckled, folded, given up – but not my Mom. When Bobbie was burned over 90% of her body at age three, all the doctors said she would never make it, but with the faith and strength of Gran Owen, her mother, she stayed bedside Bobbie, reading Bible stories, put her into God's hands, and said, "Thy will be done."

Now in my book, that is not giving up. That is letting go with faith that whatever the outcome, all is in Divine Order. After nine months in the hospital, my sister walked out, and went home to a new baby sister – me. Twelve years later, we were busy every night with a class or a concert or a rehearsal or a recital. Forget television. While we did have a TV by then, I never wanted to watch anything but the Mickey Mouse Club right after school. We always ate dinner together, then off we went to real life – a whirlwind of music, dance and theatre.

Mom never pushed me into any of this activity. I thrived on it and never thought of her as a stage mother, she just wanted us all to have opportunities she never had. Bobbie got a scholarship for piano lessons. I got a scholarship for ballet and violin. My brother learned French Horn at school, and played in Denver's Junior Police Band. I was in All City Orchestras throughout elementary school. At the age of ten, Bobbie was touring as Dr. Antonia Brico's child prodigy, destined for the concert stage. Mom was so proud. None of us had a clue how much pressure they were putting on Bobbie, so when she suddenly stopped playing the piano, ran off and married the boy next door at age fifteen, Mom was stunned, confused, devastated. For an eleven year old, this was all rather exciting and dramatic and I secretly had fantasies about running off to Hollywood to join the Mickey Mouse Club.

Then one night with Mom, in tears like I'd never seen her, poured out her heart to me. "Oh, Billie, Billie, promise me you will never do anything like this to me. Promise me. Promise me."

Now, I loved my mother more than life itself, and I had always wanted to be just like her when I grew up, so this really put me in your classic, text-book approach/avoidance ambivalence conflict. How could I live an exciting life like my big sister's and still make Mom happy? All I could do was swallow and peep, "Don't worry, Mom. I won't do that to you. I promise. Don't worry."

As might have been predictable, I never told Mom much of anything I ever did after that – so she wouldn't have to worry about me. She never knew that at age 19, I had to illegally terminate a pregnancy. She never knew that my first husband was controlling and abusive. She never knew that my second husband got three DUI's and we literally fled Colorado in the RV to escape. Even as adults, I couldn't risk breaking her heart – couldn't risk that she might be disappointed in me, and while I know she admired my cocky capacity for independence, sometimes she just couldn't figure out why I did the things I did. Truth be told, she was simply operating on a lot less than 100% information.

When I finally told her about the extent of abuse in my first marriage, and that I had always thought a wife had to toe the line, be submissive and try to harmonize every bad situation, she just looked at me, "Is that what you think I did, Billie Ruth?"

"Well, yeah Mom, isn't that what you did?"

"Billie Ruth, your Pop never abused me, either mentally or sexually."

"What about.....?"

"That's not the same thing. That was a mid-life crisis. We got through it."

Lack of 100% information, there I go again. I could have told her right then and there about my pregnancy. It would have been the perfect time. I could have said, 'Mom, he had me blackmailed. He knew about my pregnancy and threatened he'd tell you if I ever crossed him, and I just couldn't let that happen. You would never have forgiven me.' That's what I could have said, and she would have forgiven me, but I didn't.

This refusal to communicate paralyzed me. The misguided fear that I would break her heart by breaking up a bad marriage succeeded only in cementing decades of deceit. Like building a brick wall, each brick sealing one lie on top of another, until now almost two years after her death, my soul is still stuck in that murky glue; set into a solid conviction that somehow I caused her to say her final goodbye. The horrible irony is, My Saint Donna did everything for me, and would have done much, much more if only she had known what I needed. I prevented Mom from being Mom.

Oh, the things we do! Oh, the things we fail to do! So, I'm sending Musashi, Mom's sixteen year old 'grand-dog,' as another companion, but more importantly as a Messenger of Truth. Dear Mom, My Saint Donna, I know I failed you and I know you have forgiven me, but now that you know everything, I really need you to be my Mom. Hold me tight, comfort me. Tell me how much you love me. Rock me in your arms. Sing "Away in the Manger" and tell me how it's all going to be all right.

Momma's Hands

Donna Owen Hopkins Ellis

©2002

Even as Momma lay in hospice care, reminding Jesus she was ready to come home, her lovely hands lay in repose across her stomach. Her fingers were well shaped and slender. Her nails had never seen a manicure, yet they shone as if buffed and curved into cuticles perfectly smooth. The backs of her hands showed corded sinews that still retained their strength and flexibility. I looked at my own hands and realized mine would never be as beautiful.

I reached for the lotion and uncapped the bottle. I loved putting lotion on her hands, stroking the soothing liquid over each finger, kneading each knuckle slightly as I moved smoothly to the next. I spoke gently to her, never really knowing if she heard me, now that her ears were listening to angel choruses. It was as if I finally had a chance to have her to myself and could speak of anything and everything I had held inside during my whole life long.

I thought I was the elder of three children until my father's mother told me the story of Georgia Marie. When I was in sixth grade, I felt the courage to ask Momma about my older sister. I had walked into the kitchen fragrant with the smells of fresh vegetables. Her back was toward me as she looked out the window toward her garden.

Her response was at first short, "Who told you about that?" But then she stopped chopping potatoes and came toward me. She took my hands in hers and led me to the kitchen table where we each sat down. "Honey, I didn't want to tell you until you were ready."

I could smell the earthy potato fragrance coming from her cool fingers and laid my head on our clasped hands to pull that smell into my nose. "I think I'm ready to hear it now, Momma. I was surprised and a little frightened when Granny Owen told me. She doesn't like you much, does she?"

I knew I was breaching territory where I really didn't belong, but Momma's willingness to stop what she was doing and speak so openly to me gave me courage.

"Well, you see Honey," she began. She cleared her throat a bit and I saw her eyes were shining with unshed tears. "Daddy and I were already older than most when we got married. We didn't even know if we could have children. But I prayed – and prayed some more. The Lord was probably tired of hearing from me on that account and we were blessed with a child."

"But it wasn't me, was it, Momma." I wanted to let her know that I was following the story and understood.

"No, my love. Her name was Georgia Marie. She was such a lovely child – perfect in every way. But she was stillborn."

"Can I put some flowers on her grave?" I asked.

"None of us will. You see your Aunt Ruth and I had gone back to Missouri so I could be with my mother when the baby came. Your Daddy came later to be with me when he heard the news about Georgia Marie. Your Daddy made a tiny casket for her and I put the little blanket I had crocheted for her inside. We didn't take her home to Colorado – instead we buried her in the same plot where my own grandparents were laid to rest."

"Your father and I were so taken by sadness – but we couldn't grieve. The church ladies and the preacher kept coming by and 'tsk-tsking' – we were smothered. Finally your father raised his voice and told them all to just go home and leave us in peace." She smiled a tiny smile before she continued. "Your Daddy didn't ever like church folk, anyways. But they sure left us alone after that! And then I was so embarrassed I had to find another church to share my worship."

Looking at Mom's hands now, I am remembering the several different churches we attended throughout my childhood. Many of the children's songs were the same and I had enjoyed Sunday School at every one of them. I had wondered at the time why we kept changing churches – now, remembering her story about Georgia Marie, I was able to place another piece into the puzzle.

I marveled how she never lost her faith – actually, it had gotten stronger over the years. The more distant Daddy grew to anything churchy the stronger was Momma's faith in the Lord. The one time Daddy had actually softened was when he donated five acres of land to Momma's church to build a retreat center for summer-time revival meetings. By that time my own family was invited to attend. My three children were so drawn by the music and the preaching that they responded to the altar call one year. I was surprised and a bit taken back – sure didn't tell my husband about it! He would have yanked them out by an ear and probably forbid them ever visiting their grandmother again!

It's strange how strong Momma's prayers were felt in my own family, but it took my husband almost thirty years before he was able to see the good in it. His own family had raised him to rely on prayer – to trust in prayer so fully that doctors were not required. And although my mother's prayers reflected a powerful faith in the Lord's healing energies – my husband was unable to understand the similarities.

When I had been married only four years, our first child was hospitalized. Momma spent many hours in the hospital with me. The child had been badly burned and was not expected to live. Daddy blamed my husband for it – too much in a hurry to cover the ash pit sufficiently. And it appeared as if my husband bought into the guilt because he never came to the hospital in all the nine months our daughter was there. Momma prayed constantly. But what no one knew – so did my husband. But because his prayers were for the perfection of the child to be revealed, he could not allow his eyes to see the imperfection.

When my husband finally admitted that Momma was probably a saint – was about the time that Daddy finally agreed that my husband was probably a pretty good man.

Momma was the original recycler. She would collect rocks from creek beds and from the side of roads on their travels. She picked up old gloves tossed away by others – even if it was only half a pair. With these odds and ends Momma and Daddy built a home across a couple of fields from the church retreat center. They laid the rock foundations for a well house and their own home as well as a short rock wall separating the back patio from the garden. The gloves were used to make the small grooves smoothing the cement between the rocks. You only needed a few good glove-fingers that would last several "smoothings."

After Daddy died, Momma moved to be with church friends in California. She had a small apartment near the beach at Oceanside. In the early 70's she was making "yarn" by cutting plastic bags in a spiral and crocheting tote bags for beach or grocery trips. She made sun bonnets and "rag" rugs out of plastic bags. Wherever she went, they were admired and orders were filled. She had everyone collecting plastic bags for her. Sometimes she'd put out the word for a certain color – Roman Meal Bread wrappers, I remember, was a favorite request.

She was always busy doing something. One year when Momma was in her 70's she rode the Greyhound bus from California to Virginia to spend time with my grown daughter – her first granddaughter – who had survived the long hospital stay as a toddler – who had just brought forth the first great granddaughter. By the time I arrived a few weeks later, my daughter was handling her preemie easily – skills learned at Momma's hands.

Momma's prayers brought many healings to family and friends – but it was Momma's personal outlook on life and everything around that made her so very special. I don't remember a time that she was not humming a hymn. Sometimes I'd ask her to name the tune and she'd have to stop and sing a few bars before she would recognize what it was. Whatever she was doing in the kitchen, in the garden – household chores or sewing something for the grandchildren. Humming or singing hymns was the accompaniment. Momma's hands were always busy – and the lilt of old time-y hymns would be a part of whatever she was doing.

* * *

The other night I was getting ready for bed, humming a hymn and brushing out my hair. Momma appeared in the mirror behind me and I felt her hands on my shoulders. I took a stuttered breath. "Momma," I told her, "I'm going to be fine. You can go on home to Jesus." And she was gone.

Unknown Legacies

Lisa Swallow

©2015

My mother's final intake of breath cut the early morning silence like a tortured snore, wheezing, rasping and rattling as it forced its way through pale cracked lips, past thick tonsils and into her otherwise still chest. It had seemed like ages since her previous breath. My daughter-in-law Meredith and I had almost gotten used to the rattle, which the Hospice nurse had said was a sign that death was eminent. But there was no getting used to the long pauses and the wondering after each one "Is this it?" "Is she gone?" "Can I cry now?"

We had a formed a circle, my left hand holding Mom's right, Meredith's right holding Mom's left, and Meredith and I holding onto each other for strength and support. Tears streamed down my face as I studied Mom's colorless face, searching vainly for any sign of consciousness. "I'm here" I whispered. The words arose not from any conscious thought but from my promise to stay with her to the end. "I love you."

Meredith squeezed my hand gently and I squeezed back. Then, before our hands could relax, a wave of energy like a faint electric shock, passed from Mom, through us, and back into her shell of a body. And rather than tensing in preparation for the next breath, her chest relaxed. It was the end of 76 years of a life lived fully. It was a surrender to the unknown.

We sat with her, silent, for several more minutes, then slowly released hands and stood, stiff from hours at her side. Meredith smiled a sweet tentative smile and we stepped towards each other into a tight hug. Meredith's arms were safe and substantial, her breathing steady and alive.

"Thank you," I whispered. "Thank you for being here."

"Thank you…" Meredith whispered back, "For letting me be here."

"I don't know why we are whispering," We looked over at Mom, impervious to whispers, and at Tiny, her toy poodle and companion who slept soundly at her feet. And then we laughed softly.

"What now?" Hospice had said we could call any time, but neither of us had any urge to do so. Mom was at peace in her own home and that felt right.

"I think we should get some sleep," Meredith said.

Calling the funeral home could wait. Saying the D word could wait. I couldn't even cry yet, couldn't break the 3 am silence or focus on my own pain. Technically, clinically, it was over, but it was still Mom's time.

"I failed." Mom had said just a week ago. "I wasn't brave enough. I just couldn't do it."

"Failed at what?" I had asked, incredulously.

"My whole life, I felt I'd been put here for a reason," she said. "I was supposed to do something. Something important. That's why I didn't have the biopsy sooner. I was sure that lump couldn't be serious because I hadn't done it yet. I still wasn't even sure what I was supposed to do."

In her sadness she looked like a grief stricken child. Disbelief mingled with loss and puzzlement. "I was supposed to do something. Something that would have made it all worth while."

I knew the "all" she was referring to was the abuse she had suffered as a child then later as an adult. The hardship and hunger of poverty…

The loneliness of divorce. I had held her, feeling her sorrow and her fear.

"I don't see you as a failure," I had said, stroking her hair. "You did so much for so very many people."

My mother had dedicated her life to serving others, first as a teacher, then as a marriage, family, and child counselor. She had had an unquenchable thirst for learning. Buddha, Christ, Lao Tse sat side by side on the bookcase in her office. Bookcases in other rooms bulged with works on metaphysics, New Age thought, neurological development and all forms of healing.

"And you did so much. You came so far," I whispered. "Most of all, you set an example for us. You lit the way."

As soon as I heard my own words, I knew them to be true.

Yet, I understood what she meant when she declared herself a failure. Try as she might, she had never succeeded in learning to love herself and never escaped the fear that perhaps she just wasn't "good enough" to know God.

Throughout her last days I pondered her "failure," and asked myself what my words to her had really meant. I searched for a way to let her see herself through my eyes and grasped for the words that would explain just how important her gifts to me really were.

But most of all I wanted to let her know that over the past few months something had shifted inside me and I was not the person I had been. As I looked within myself I saw that I was almost ashamed that through her death something awesome and wonderful was sparked in me.

Mom had spent her entire life chasing after happiness, safety, and ease. They had been a rainbow for her, in sight so much of the time but never attainable. Yet somehow, miraculously, I had gotten a glimpse of all those things while sharing her last few months with her. Without knowing it, she had led me to the pot of gold and let me dip my hands into the treasure of pain and laughter, connection, and loss.

And now it was my job to piece those glimpses together into a path. But for now it was time to be with her, with her absence and with....

Close a book and sit quietly, feeling the richness of her life and the finality of her death. There would be plenty of time for the mourning, for the tears. For now, while we could still feel her presence, I needed to sit in awe and respect as she passed.

My life would never be the same again, and not just because my mother was gone.

I hadn't been aware of it at the time, but Mom's diagnosis of Stage 4 Metastatic Breast cancer had jolted me awake for the first time in decades; jolted me into the awareness that I must remember to celebrate life, be open to the beauty, and to take every breath living each moment to the fullest.

Chapter Four

REGRETS? PERHAPS— BUT THERE ARE NO DO-OVERS

OTHERWISE KNOWN AS:

Letting Go

*I learned to forgive myself, and that enabled me
to forgive my mother as a person.*

– Amy Tan

When we let go of the resentment and keeping score, we realize that what is – IS and that's the way it will remain. We can move on from here, but only if we accept that our mother did the best she could under the circumstances – forgive her and forgive ourselves for holding on so long to the hurt.

There may be no "do-overs" – but there will be opportunities where we can make amends...

When she comes to us in our dreams...

When we hear her voice in our minds...

When we sense her presence...

We know that Love is an active verb – we can continue to pass it along.

AND Love is an indestructible essence of being-ness – Love endures.

Even if she is no longer on this earth, the resonances of her presence has been felt by others – others who will continue to say that you remind them of her… and wanting to play ' remember when's.' Breathe in these comments as a blessing to you – feel your mother's spirit lingering near – and simply know that

Mothers are for always, quirks and all.

Brownie and Forgiveness

Bobbie Hopkins Spivey

©2006

Brownie was a bear. But not just any old bear. Brownie was special. A nurse brought him to me when another child in the ward at Denver's Children's Hospital did not make it through the night. I was three years old; but I immediately recognized that Brownie was lonesome. I held him close, all that day, whispering to him that everything was going to be all right. Nine months later, I was released to come home. Brownie did not travel in the box of medical supplies that went home with me. We had become fast friends and companions. Brownie was tight in my arms. The doctors and nurses had done all they could do. Some said it was a miracle that I had even lived. Others stated that I would probably never walk. Since I was four years old, these words were never spoken to me.

I was plagued with very bad dreams while in the hospital and for many years afterward. Brownie taught me to rely on his presence to scare away the creatures that came out of the forest, or from under the bed. In my dreams, Brownie would come alive and assume full size. All he needed to do was stand on his two hind legs and roar, and the scary monsters would run away.

Bad dreams are apparently an expected by-product of ether, the anesthesia used during the period after WWII. I had seven surgeries to graft small pieces of skin from my chest, buttocks and hips to burned areas of my legs. The technique used was called "pinch grafting." It encouraged healthy skin to grow in and around the "pinches" and connect the tissue to make a whole new fabric of skin. The ether used during those surgeries stayed in my system for many years. Clinically, I know that what I shared with Brownie were lucid dreams. But at the time those dreams were powerful examples to my young mind – *my thoughts are strong enough to control the outcome of any situation.* With Brownie in my arms, the bad dreams became adventures. I was confident at all times that together we would be champions, defeating and overcoming all the bad guys. And an unexpected benefit of the ether in my system was that mosquitoes avoided me until I was in my twenties.

Shortly after I turned four, I was sent home from the hospital. We made the transition home with courage. While I had been gone, a new baby sister had arrived; the bedroom I shared with my little brother was not the same. Because my mother was nursing my baby sister, and because my grandmother was a practical nurse, I was to stay with my grandmother. Brownie reminded me that he was there with me and that I did not need to be afraid.

One morning I was lying in bed in my grandparents' Florida room, with the sunshine streaming through the sheers at all the windows; and a voice spoke to me from the sliding glass doorway. I looked in that direction and saw two figures, wearing white robes. They were back-lit by the sunlight and details of their features were not very clear. One called me by name and asked me to come with them. I was willing to do so, but told them I had to get my slippers on the floor by the other side of the bed. I slipped off the bed and put on my slippers. When I stood up and reached for Brownie, the men were gone.

No one in my family thought the story was strange. But I made the mistake of sharing it with my third grade class, a few years later. Eight year olds in a public school classroom should not be asked to accept intangibles during a "show and tell." My adult mind revisiting that incident reminds me that I was not ready to leave this earthly plane. Brownie and my slippers were the tangible items that kept me from transitioning.

Over the years and throughout many moves our family made, Brownie became a constant accessory to my bedroom decor. I know that my mother saw him as a stuffed animal. I never felt it necessary to share our secret that he could come alive when I needed him to. Especially after the fiasco with the "show and tell," I had learned to keep private things private. Brownie was more than a friend and companion. Keeping him close, resting under my chin, I had transferred many tears to his furry head. His ears had been stroked and caressed as I gazed into his eyes and told him about my day at school or play. Even as this show of affection took the hair from his head and left his ears thin and threadbare, he was my Love. So, the morning I found that my loving him had separated Brownie's head from his body during the night, I did not think I had to specifically request that he be left alone until I could put him back together. I tried that morning, with the little time I had. The hard neck ring would not give enough to push the fabric of the head back inside it. Mother called from the kitchen that I would be late for school if I didn't hurry. I gently laid Brownie back on the bed and felt sick to my stomach to see the finely shaved wood straw that filled his chest cavity.

We lived in Springfield, Colorado – the most southeastern corner of the state. Springfield was a wonderful adventure for me. I rode my bicycle all over; I played touch football with the boys down the street. Walking to school was a wonderful experience because I could walk down the alley behind several barnyards on my way. Talking with the horses, cows and sheep in their paddocks was the best part of the walk. Because of my relationship to Brownie, I believed completely that I could communicate with all the animals. They always greeted me when I spoke with them. I had learned to whinny, moo and baa so that my nine-year-old ears heard identical sounds within their replies.

When I returned from school that day, I headed straight for my bedroom to help Brownie. He was not on my bed where I had left him. I looked under the bed, back against the wall, in the closet and everywhere I could think he might be. I finally asked my mother.

"Mom, have you seen Brownie? I can't find him!"

"Well, honey. His head came off. I put him in the trash."

Maybe it was not spoken in such a short and cursory manner. But the impact was brutal. I ran outside to the trash bin; but I was too late. It had been picked up that day while I was in school. Trash in Springfield was hauled fifty miles away to the large dump in Lamar. Brownie was gone.

I cried for days, and would not speak to my mother for a very long time. She apologized profusely and often. I believe she even cried with me several times. But there was nothing either of us could do about it.

Throughout my life, I would tell this story. Always in the presence of my mother, so that she could feel ashamed again. I was quite adept at making it sound like a funny story and listeners would laugh. My mother would try to smooth over the tension she knew I felt by again apologizing. I would tell her I knew she was sorry.... But I never accepted her apologies, nor did I tell her I forgave her. I did not forgive her. I could not forgive her.

Brownie didn't look like any bear I've ever seen. His golden brown fur was silky soft. He had arms that curved to suggest an elbow and legs that were long. His arms and legs swiveled in their sockets so that he could sit or stand, reach for you or "reach for the sky." He was an elegant bear of perfect posture. And when he spoke, his voice was modulated and cultured.

My home and office are filled with bears of various sizes, shapes and attire. Many of these are gifts from my friends and family, who were under the impression that I collect bears. In reality, I have been searching all this time for a duplicate. The closest I've come to seeing Brownie again was a series of stamps named "the teddy bear collection," put out by the United States Postal Service when postage was thirty-two cents. There he sits in one of the frames, tilted forward toward his right leg, head inclined to the same angle, downcast face. Lonesome. Seeing this stamp, my hopes were renewed. He was out there, somewhere, because the post office had his picture. I got on the web and searched for hours, and for days. Each hint of finding Brownie was a dead end. I spent fifty dollars on a chance that one of them shipped from England would be Brownie. It arrived, course hair and humped. The color wasn't even right.

Then Beanie Babies put out their edition of the golden brown teddy named "Fuzz." It wasn't Brownie, but it was so close! So, so close. And the feel of his fur was soft, the color was perfect. And he had long arms and long legs. I held him to my face and blinked back the tears. I couldn't move, nor speak. Here I was, a grown woman with grown children of my own, standing in the back of that Hallmark store, feeling the flush of love rushing through my whole body. I heard his voice again. Not from this tiny Beanie Baby I held to my face – but Brownie of my heart and mind spoke to me.

I purchased one for my mother. It was almost Christmas, and her birthday was near too. Fuzz/Brownie would be a loving gesture to my mother. Brownie dictated a note that I put in the box. I do not remember exactly what it said. But it was an apology for holding my mother "hostage" with the Brownie Story. And it was a belated request to forgive me for not forgiving her for all those years.

That Christmas, when my mother opened her Brownie gift, there were tears in her eyes. There was also a sweet smile on her lips AND an impish glow over all her face.

"What is it, Mom?" I asked.

"I'll tell you later. Open your gift."

As I rustled the wrapping and reached into the box I felt a soft and silky, scrunchy thing.

"Do you forgive me, now?" she asked.

I should have known. For a tiny moment, I was still childish enough to think my mother was not capable of an identical love and forgiving nature as I had shown. But it was for just a tiny moment. Love blesses us all in wonderful ways we will never hope to duplicate without it. In my box sat an identical Beanie Baby Fuzz/Brownie. We laughed and cried together. And had an even better story to share the next time we were with friends.

Death and Duck Feet

Nina Boyd Krebs

©2006

The budget process bumped along, debate swayed from one side of the table to the other. Department heads in the Student Affairs Division sorted through priorities and special interests deciding how to spend the year's funds. Never a favorite part of my job as Director of the Counseling Center, I fought drowsiness and distraction. Thoughts of what to fix for supper, or when I could take Karen and Erica shopping, easily robbed my attention from number columns and influence trading.

Dave's face passed the reflecting glass rectangle in the closed door. *Odd*, I thought, but not totally off the wall since he worked at the Counseling Center too. But he had no reason to be in this building. Then he opened the door and walked into the room.

He motioned for me to come into the hallway, interrupting the meeting in process. Agitated, I wondered what could be so important. I still didn't get it. Then I did. Something serious had happened. Adrenalin erased my drowsiness.

"I just took a call from Judy," he said. His cloudy green eyes and unsmiling mouth warned me. "I'm sorry to tell you this, Honey," he hesitated and took my hand, "your mother has died."

No tears came. No wave of sadness. I didn't know what to feel. My body snapped taut and my brain clicked into calculating arrangements – work coverage, child care, air fare. Who would finish the budget?

Yet, no thanks to my thoughts or conscious awareness, something shifted deep inside. A dark interior revolution edged into layers of insulation. "Mother is dead. I should cry," echoed in my mind. My world had changed. I couldn't tell how.

A dreamlike walk across campus to my office gave me time to think about what to do and wonder what I would say to my sister, Judy. I knew that I would go to Phoenix to the funeral. Beyond that, I had no plans.

Mother had been enraged that Dave and I lived together for a couple years before we married. "He's just after your money," she had hissed at me bitterly. Dave held rank as a full professor with a salary half again as large as mine. My entry level job, student loans, and two young daughters suspended me on an economic tight rope. Mother thought that "doctor" meant "wealthy."

Dave had no experience with my mother other than as target for her hostility. Why she hated him so much, I had no idea. He saw nothing of her but her rage and was the first person to point out, much to my shock, what an angry woman she was.

Knowing his feelings, I insisted that I could go to Phoenix by myself.

"I'd like to go with you," he urged, wisely and generously. "My relationship with your family doesn't matter. I can be your friend. It will help to have an outsider." I gratefully melted into relief that he would be there for me.

Exposing someone I loved to the constrained convolutions of human pain I knew would be waiting felt brutal. Around my family, long-standing rules against honest talk dug into me like rusted spikes that twisted when I tried to move around them. My anxiety skyrocketed. Years of distance made the thought of squeezing back into the suffocating silence feel like shrinking myself into the tiny image at the wrong end of a telescope.

The little tract house on Indianola Avenue in Phoenix had never been my home. I'd visited a few times and felt the bittersweet pull of leftovers from my childhood. Mother's treasured "Rebecca at the Well" sculpture, her prized silver coffee service, the blown glass deer, and Grandmother Boyd's Haviland china still inhabited walnut corner cabinets. Assorted kachinas, a de Grazia print, fuchsia, red and purple Mexican candle holders brightened living areas. Familiar dishes, colorful serving pieces, neatly folded linens, and other household necessities, many I remembered from my young life, crammed closets and cupboards. Some of the furniture I'd seen, some I hadn't, but the house offered the whimsically artistic touches Mother managed in the vortex of pain that spun her life. Her pansies bloomed off the backyard patio. The mirage of love and comfort hooked me on *home*.

In some conversation with the friend who had discovered Mother's body, I mentioned that Dave and I were planning to move to a hotel.

"Please don't do that," she implored. "It would mean a lot to your mother for both you and Judy to stay here tonight."

Through the turmoil, another thread pulled at my consciousness. What had been the cause of Mother's death? Because of her medical history, it was easy to guess that she had a stroke. But what specifically had happened? Did she die alone? Had they had one last yelling match?

My father could get around, barely, with the aid of a walker. I couldn't tell how much he could see or comprehend. He'd made a life work of helplessness, so he must be frightened as well as bereft. Long-standing lack of communication had erased my capacity to guess, so I had no way to know. I could hardly stand to look at him, and felt like the ultimate jerk for harboring vengeance toward someone so pitiful. Predictably, my father had nothing to say.

"You must be very sad," I said to him, after we'd been there a while, taking responsibility to attempt some connection. He glared at me. Did he hear me? Did it make any difference to him that I was there? I knew him so little, his reaction held only mystery.

He didn't reply.

The day moved on. Judy and I dazedly took clothing to the mortuary, chose a casket, made arrangements for a service. Feeling alien and intrusive, I urged Judy to make most of the decisions. One of Mother's few specific requests was to be buried at the Eastern Star Cemetery. Judy took care of it.

Sitting in the living room, a few old friends watched the day go by with the scanty remains of a nearly extinct family. Death, duty, destiny unfolded. Sadness about Mother's life put its foot in my chest and stopped words and breath. Tears balked. Dry pain froze me.

Several times bits of conversations were started by one or another of those sitting around, but never picked up. What did they want to talk about? What could be said? We couldn't exactly say that Babe had such an unhappy life she quit taking her blood pressure medicine and almost immediately died a horrible death? We couldn't say that Hugh is such a pitiful creature he won't live long without Babe who abdicated herself to his needs in exchange for the "security" he provided. People continued to come and go, saying very little to each other. Eventually, we all went to bed.

The next morning we continued funeral planning details, tip-toeing around the concept of "what next." Judy declared she wanted to bring Dad back with her to live with her family. My immediate reaction was one of relief. But it was quickly replaced with pictures of what that could be like for my two teenage nephews.

"Let's think about that, Judy," I begged. "We don't want to make too hasty a decision."

A little after noon, I could stay in the house no longer, and asked Dave to accompany me. I knew a wonderful Chinese restaurant not far away and thought a tasty lunch in a quiet, foreign place might help. The elegant restaurant, nearly empty, offered respite. Too many waiters seated us, brought menus and invited our orders. It took a long time to make my brain move between the Chinese translations in the complicated menu and decide on a duck dish that sounded interesting.

In silence that was finally comfortable, we awaited our meal. Dave had ordered chow mein which the waiters elegantly arranged on his plate. Then they stepped back, eyes cast downward. The senior server lifted the cover of the tureen he had placed before me, releasing spicy vapors that juiced my numbed salivary glands. Yes, duck had been a good decision.

Gradually, my eyes focused on the contents. Arranged in a perfect spiral on the flat-bottomed vessel, stood approximately one dozen beautifully cooked duck feet, a short portion of each leg ascending like a little pole from its webby base.

During World War II my parents had owned and operated a chicken ranch. Sometimes mother cleaned and cooked chicken feet – saying that some people considered them a delicacy. In my confused state, eating duck feet had assumed real possibilities.

"Nina," Dave urged gently, "I can tell from the look on your face you don't want to eat that. You don't have to."

Finally, I cried. I didn't have to keep it together any more. The waiter tactfully departed, lid in hand.

The day after the funeral, Dave and I moved to the Westward Ho Hotel – a comforting place in a reminiscent way. I had thought it was the ultimate in luxury when at age twelve, I came to Phoenix to represent Navajo County in the state Spelling Bee and it was the biggest hotel in town. I had misspelled "haggard," or does it just have one "g"? in an early round ending my pubescent moment in fame. The innocence of that time and the purity of its pain and my shame at failure engulfed me as I walked into the worn lobby. Childhood seemed light years behind me. That night, snuggled in Dave's arms, my decision was easy. I would release my share of whatever inheritance there was, and help move Dad into a nursing home in Phoenix. I would propose this to Judy in the morning.

On the last pass through the house, when I went back to say goodbye to Daddy and Judy, I picked up a Hopi basket that had been the waste-basket under my desk when I was a child in Winslow. I added two Hopi plaques, some other small pieces, including my rattle with most of the paint worn off, and two kachina dolls. Probably all of these things had been given to Mother by Meme.

Everything I wanted to claim from my past, my inheritance, fit under the seat in the plane for my flight home.

In Tribute To Grace Hinkley Sanderson

Betty Sanderson Owen

©2006

My first conscious memory of my mother is very clear. I can see her sitting at her dressing table, and my small three-year-old self standing near her. Our conversation eludes me but I remember my mother looking down at me and saying, "You are adorable!"

This memory shines in my mind to this day, and I wonder at that, because I don't think I could possibly have understood the meaning of the words, but my mother's smile, and the love in her eyes, burned into my small soul, and her message remains.

My mother was born at the end of the Victorian age, and grew up in the early 1900's, coming into young womanhood at the dawn of the roaring 20's. She confided to my daughter one day (not to me) how difficult it was for her to try to conceal her bountiful bosom when the flat-chested "flapper" styles were in fashion. I have the tattered remains of her wedding dress, and indeed, it was the typical long-waisted flapper design. How I would love to have a picture of my mother wearing it! Alas, there were no wedding photos.

In that bygone era many things were just not discussed, and often my mother exhibited a faint disgust for all things pertaining to the human body. Her ability to dress herself in the mornings totally beneath and within the confines of her nightgown was to me an amazing feat. She would take her arms out of the sleeves and hook up her corset and brassiere, maneuvering deftly beneath her gown, and then voila, the nightgown would drop around her feet, and there she stood, in her slip, ready to put on her dress. I still don't know how she did it.

The closest I ever came to seeing my mother's body was at the Lakeside amusement park in Denver. We were on a family outing one summer day and my mother was taking a short rest on a park bench when an ant crawled up under her dress and bit her. She came unglued, yanked her dress up and clawed at herself in some of the most un-ladylike contortions. My dad nearly fell off the bench laughing, but it really was not funny because Mother was highly allergic to insect bites. But Dad hee-hawed until Mother lit into him and put the fear of the Lord in him. It rather quenched the spirit of the day. When Mama ain't happy, ain't nobody happy!

I was a good natured, happy child, but timid, too, so I do not remember many conflicts with my mother. I always tried to please, and most of the time I did, but kids will be kids. My brother and I were required to do the supper dishes, a chore he hated but reluctantly did until my sister was old enough to take his place. One night we were standing at the kitchen sink, and we could see Mother and Dad sitting in the dimly lighted living room. I, with some strange reverse logic, thought that, because they were sitting in the dark, they could not see me, and I stuck out my tongue at them, just to see what would happen. Well, all heck broke loose, and I learned an important lesson in physics that night.

My parents had an odd notion that to be too forthcoming with praise might somehow cause children to become arrogant and prideful, so they had a devious way of dealing with that problem. They would be lavish in their praise of my siblings, to me, and equally lavish in their praise of me, to them. This scheme backfired. The result was that we each thought that Mother and Dad loved "the others" best. My sister and I were grown before we confessed to each other these secrets. I grew up thinking that my parents greatly admired my sister's "spit-fire" spirit, which made me all the more aware of my timid nature. All the while my sister got an ear-full of my admirable qualities, and she thought Mother and Dad admired me more. What a perverse way to compliment your children! How far we have come in the area of child psychology since those days!

I have pondered on the subtleties of family love. My family was not kissy-huggy. Although I would have benefited from a little more positive feedback, there was always an underlying feeling of security, an undercurrent of safety that I could not have defined or described. As Dr. Phil would put it, home was always a soft place to fall.

My mother tutored my father while he was a student at Colorado Agricultural College, after World War I, and she herself had spent the war years teaching school in the little mountain towns of Kremmling and Dillon. During the lean depression years when jobs were almost nonexistent, my dad used his landscaping skills to make a living.

Between the two of them they transformed the little acre around our tiny two-room house into a garden show-place. My mother's flower-beds were something to behold! It was from her I learned the names of all the flowers and plants, and to identify the song birds in our yard. We ate from our vegetable garden, and from my mother I learned the art of canning and preserving, and jam and jelly making. My parents made this a fun family activity. I can still see my dad in his big white apron, up to his elbows in suds, scalding fruit jars.

The depression years were tough on my parents, yet we children did not ever feel deprived. I look back on a full, rich childhood.

My mother loved language and poetry and in the right situation could have been a writer. She insisted that we speak proper grammar even among ourselves at home, and we children became very quick to criticize those who didn't. She was our mother, but she was first and foremost a teacher.

If my mother had a fault, it was that she had difficulty communicating her love in physical ways, but if love is there it will find a way.

Joie De Vivre: A French-Canadian Inheritance

Roseanna Frechette

©1993

Although I was born in the United States, I have always been happy to tell people I am French-canadian. *Joie de Vivre,* I say and then smile. The joy of being alive is a precious gift I inherited. Of this, I am sure. From Aline Charlotte Vezina came my spirited, adventuresome ability to 'go for it' in life.

Aline was the daughter of musician, Raoul Vezina and grand daughter of Quebec Symphony composer and conductor, Joseph Vezina. She was initially raised, after the death of her mother, by a great aunt on the third floor of a quaint store front on Quebec's Huron Street. At a young age she entered boarding school where English was primary. She later attended the French university to become a nurse. During World War II, Aline Charlotte Vezina brought her inherent passion for life to the United States. She answered a Red Cross recruit in the Chicago area and was placed in the French-Canadian community of Kankakee, Illinois, where she met my father, Frigon Lou Frechette, a musician also of French-Canadian descent. Their passionate love for one another led to a marriage which gradually coupled the *joie de vivre* factor into a rather large Catholic family of 13 Frechettes.

I am the ninth child of Aline and Frigon. Throughout my childhood, I learned over and over that, although *joie de vivre* literally translates into 'joy of living,' what it really means is a zest and a spirit for life, an ability to embrace fully the experience of being alive in good times and bad. My early memory of our home is full with excitement and chaos, conflict and peace, as well as the things it takes to grow a family of so many under one roof.

Meal time was important family time, sitting around a monstrous table, we conversed while we ate. We took turns washing and drying piles of dishes and got to know each other in the process. Music was with us always. In fact, the house saw no day go by without live music being played. We heard Daddy on the organ; Madeleine, Margaret, Joseph, Pauline, Lea, and Christopher taking turns on piano; Philip, Joseph and David on guitars; Robert with trumpet or drums; Pauline played the violin, too. Alice and I joined in singing. Even though my father had taught me piano, I always preferred just to sing, hearing my voice like a musical instrument. Mom sang, too. And she listened, giving a lion's share of encouragement to our talents.

When our television broke, my mother refused to replace it. "If you want entertainment," she insisted, "read." I won every book report contest of my grade school years. Books were far more satisfying to my adventuresome appetite than watching situation comedy and popular violence so often the focus of TV. To this day, I devour books and watch very little television.

My mother's insistence that we live, rather than sit back and watch life, was evident in the ways she encouraged us to participate in everything we felt passionate about. Our family always had two or more performers on various stages at once. During my early adolescence, we sang as one choir. Eleven children. Eleven voices. We hit all the ranges with harmonies; my father at the big Wurlitzer organ in the bank lobby. Christmas shoppers came and went as we sang Mother's favorite French Christmas Carols from her treasured record, "Christmas in France." As I sang these French words, many of which I had no English meaning for, I sang my heritage, my *joie de vivre*. I seemed to know what the words meant just by singing them with full voice and heart.

Financial reality for the wife of a self-employed musician with 11 children left Aline little if any time for leisure and no means for travel out of our region. Only once that I recall did she journey back to her native land. It was for her stepmother's funeral. And when she returned, she was the happiest I'd ever seen her. She brought gifts of maple sugar, maps of her province, and artwork depicting the streets of Quebec in line drawings and water colors. We hung these pictures about the house, and although I've not actually visited all the places they depicted, I seem to know them all well.

Small things brought her joy in the face of hard life: Pralines made with real maple sugar; her twins (myself and my brother) marching in the same high school band; watching new snowfall as it muffles street noise; rocking in her easy chair while listening to one of us play classical piano. Mother even loved to clean the venetian blinds, listening to "My Fair Lady" on a scratchy old Victrola. These were all things my mother knew to cherish, along with the return of a son from Viet Nam, and the birth of a grandchild. And, of course, her traditional Christmas Eve midnight feast. *"Le Reveillon."*

No matter what the hardship of the particular year, she always managed to produce celebrated *Le Reveillon*. I remember them quite clearly. It makes sense that this Christmas holiday event prevailed in my mother's house, as it represented food, family, and celebration, all elements of great priority to the Quebecois. On Christmas Eve, those who were old enough would attend Midnight Mass, oftentimes singing in the choir as my father accompanied on pipe organ. Once home from church, the meal that Mother had prepared in phases all day would be enjoyed.

A table set with colorful Christmas linen, china, crystal, silver, a great platter loaded with a huge turkey, often weighing 25 or more pounds, and stuffed with my mother's secret dressing. Gravy, two kinds of potato, two or three kinds of bread, fresh green beans, cranberries, homemade fruitcake. The food was much like what we saw at Thanksgiving. But we were eating after midnight with candlelight as if we were royalty, sipping wine and after-dinner brandy.

Then came our gift exchange around the Christmas tree. Those children who weren't old enough to participate in mass and dinner were now awakened for the long, exciting process of unwrapping a mountain of treasures given heartfully from one to another. It was an all-night party, this great family fun in the spirit of Christmas! I love to recall my first experience of participating fully in *Le Reveillon*. A rite of passage, it not only marked my entry into young adulthood, but firmly established my root connection to a French-Canadian heritage.

Aline Vezina embraced life as it led her to the U.S. Midwest, my father, my siblings, myself. Every day for 17 years, with few exceptions, my mother was in my life. Her essence touches me still. Out of her roots, grew mine. My life would not be the same were it not for Mom's *joie de vivre*. I will always have her 'go for it' attitude.

When the tragedy of my mother's premature death shrouded me in a veil of ice, I heard the warm voice of my ancestors calling me to Canada. The year was 1973. I was 17. I took six weeks away from the nearly empty nest our house had become. I left my school work in search of a way to begin healing my heart. I journeyed to Quebec. While staying with my mother's youngest sister, Marthe, and her family in a renovated farmhouse near the Saint Lawrence seaway, I discovered a tree house overlooking the water. From there, I began to understand my deep need for nature that two years later landed me in Colorado. I was absorbing the landscape of my mother's life.

It was the very spirit for life I received from my mother that finally brought me the power to fully grieve the loss of her some years later. In a cathartic Caribbean island adventure I most permanently healed the chronic wound that losing my mother so many years earlier had caused. While dancing alone on a wild, rugged strip of Atlantic beach, I became acutely aware of Aline Charlotte Vezina. The pain of losing her and the power of having been her daughter animated me to fits. I wailed into the waves. Singing, crying, and moaning as I leaped, lunged, sashayed, and spun along the sandy shoreline. I was able to embrace my pain as never before. Ecstatically, I absorbed the beauty all around. In those moments, I became *Joie de Vivre*.

YOUR OCEAN

Roseanna Frechette

©December 13, 1993

(for my mother, Aline Vezina)

I went to the ocean
and there I found you
your spirit, a wave
rolling
grief bank
swept over me
dancing and prancing
on sand
singing song of
abandoned one.
I know that you
never hoped to leave
us motherless
all your children
continue to grieve
loss of you
French-Canadian woman
who journeyed
away from her
native ground
found mate
some fifty-odd years
and a soul song ago.

People say you died young
but for you
life was old
old as I always
knew you to be
never young
to the 9th child
could see
what a big price you paid
for eleven of us that you fed
bathed and nursed
through long nights
of our childhood illnesses
nightmares.
I always felt special
when sickness
befell me
because you were
not only
mother but nurse
who'd left lovely Quebec
for the US Midwest
where you put
care you could
into home.

I'm still nursing the wound
that your death
gave to me
sometimes pour from it
buckets of tears like soft
rainwater falling
in grey sheets to cleanse.
Every year early on in December

I turn a blue hue
while the sad
17-year-old
girl in me
cries out
for mother she lost
in the night 20 years
from this day
counting back
through all Christmases
we knew without you.

Count back
past the times
you weren't there
to the times that you were
making sure
Santa Claus came
though mostly on wish and a prayer
on a shoestring
he came bringing
mythical sleighful of
gifts wrapped in love
of your offspring
an oversized brood
that sang out
the French carols you taught us
tradition you loved
and passed on
like the *Reveillon*
midnight feast following
Catholic mass Christmas eve
something you brought
from the province

you never forgot
like the wedding vows
seen in a worn band of gold
I am wearing
been wearing
for 20 years counting back
seasons of your life
held strong bonds
did not lose their strength
when the times held
confusion and chaos
or poverty crosses to bear.

Joie de vivre was there
underneath all your worries
your birthright shown through
like the desert rose
short-lived but packed
with such beauty
your smile
and laughter so charged
with a spirit for life
that you passed on
to us
one by one
each by each
from the sidelines
of chronic depression
that weight on your back
not too heavy
for coaching your kids:
find the way
set your sight

field your dreams.
And believe you we did
you believed every
one of us
carried your birthright
so right you were
still are
in memories
visit
roll forward
like waves
counting back
to the lifetime
we saw as
your ocean.

Same ocean
that mothers me now
brought me conch shell
in shape of a female
torso to honor
the day
when I'd journeyed
from US Midwest
to West Indian seaside
and found you
Aline Vezina
found your ocean
your spirit, a wave.

Mama, Help Me Understand

Lisa Swallow

©2015

I don't remember why I decided to go to therapy in my late twenties. Mine had been a normal childhood: Campfire Girls, 4H and best friends punctuated by birthday parties, teen idol crushes and the prom. Except for a few bumps in the road, like my parents' divorce and my father's death when I was nine, my life had been easy. Or so I thought.

The first thing I learned in therapy was how out of touch I was with my emotions. I had always been an avid reader, so I had a huge "feeling" vocabulary, but my experience of feelings was mostly in my head. It took two years of play therapy in a safe environment to let myself feel sadness, grief, resentment, and finally, joy.

The second thing I learned was that my life had not been normal, nor had it been easy. It turns out, most girls didn't know how to mix seven types of cocktails by the time they are 12 and most girls don't dress in layers to keep their step-father and his drunk friends from making inappropriate remarks. It turns out some kids don't get punished for breaking a glass or laughing too loudly, and many children are told they are loved.

My mother loved me. I never doubted that, but she didn't keep me safe and she rarely put the needs of her children before her own. The hurting little child inside me wanted to know why. I needed to understand.

After two years of therapy, I took advantage of a quiet moment on Thanksgiving Day after the meal was over and dishes done. She was knitting in the big chair. I was flat on my back, Nick and Kit having just run off after using me as a jungle gym.

"So, Mom," I began. "Sometimes when I watch the kids play, I get this swelling in my heart. I love them so much. I feel blessed to have them in my life."

"That sounds nice."

"I was wondering... Did you ever feel anything like that for me?"

Mom looked up and met my eye for the barest of instants. "No." She looked away.

Was that sadness I'd seen in her eyes? Or regret? Or was my own sadness reflecting back at me? I lay on the floor staring at the ceiling a long while, then slowly I got up and wandered to the other room where the kids were playing.

I never asked Mom about her feelings for me again. Now and then, though, I would slip in a question or two about the past. "Why did we only get a birthday party every three years?" My brother and sister and I took turns, so for each of us our parties fell on birthdays divisible by three.

"I never had a birthday party," Mom replied. "I guess I didn't know what was normal. I thought I was doing good with one a year."

And there it was, the first clue. A few weeks later I asked another question. "Why didn't you go to college?"

"Money. I had a scholarship, but I couldn't afford the books."

Then another, "I thought you lived in Kansas when you were growing up. But just now you mentioned Ohio."

"My father remarried. His new wife wanted kids but wasn't getting pregnant. So they sent for us girls. Mama thought we'd have a better life, so she let us go."

"And…"

"We lived with them for a few years, until our step-momma started having babies. Then they sent us back home."

"Did you like it there?"

I swear, a dark cloud really did pass over her face. "No."

She'd let little things slip, but, when I asked follow up questions, quickly turned the discussion to something current. A picture was starting to form in my mind, but not nearly as quickly as I needed. Then a simple little question led to the discovery that my Grandma was willing to talk.

"Grandma, what's your middle name?"

"I don't have one."

"What?"

"Well, my mother didn't want me. From the time she first discovered she was pregnant, she did everything she could to make me miscarry. It didn't work. Then late in her pregnancy, she finally got her wish, but I didn't die. I was tiny. Less than two pounds. My mother would have left me to die except for the neighbor lady who was there at the birth. She put me in a shoebox and stuck me in the warming oven on the side of the old wood stove. She came by every day to make sure they were feeding me. My mother didn't even want to give me a name so the neighbor lady did. She called me Marguerite. After the flower, I guess. But my mother refused to give me a middle name because she didn't think I needed one. She was still hoping I would die."

Oh… My… God.

Grandma didn't mind talking about the past, at least not now that I was grown. I, on the other hand, found I could only take her story in bits and pieces. Every little bit shocked. Every little bit hurt for that little girl that she'd been. Over time Grandma helped me piece together a picture of my heritage. Meanwhile, Mom kept dropping little tidbits of her own.

Grandma was the fourth of five children. Her mother wanted all the others, just not her. Grandma's life hadn't gotten any easier when she grew up and left home. Faced with staying with the abusive father of her two children, or raising them on her own, she chose the latter, hoping to keep them safe.

It was the middle of the Depression, and they were poor, living in a tiny house in the country with an actual dirt floor. Grandma hadn't finished high school. She grew flowers and vegetables for seeds, which she sold to supplement the income from her various odd jobs. Twice she'd had run out of money for food, and resorted to taking the two girls to the Children's home, where they could be clothed and fed for a time. Mama never told her about the big man and the dark closet. When her ex-husband asked to take the girls, she believed his new wife had changed him, somehow soothed the beast that had raged in him when he'd been with her. She had been wrong.

Over time, as more stories unfolded, I came to understand.

My mother had loved us and cared for us as best she could. Measured against her own childhood, she'd done a great job. She never sent us away, never let us forget that we had a place with her... a home.

Healing takes time. In our case, it has taken generations. Finally, though, we have learned what it means to be safe and to feel love.

AUTHOR BIOGRAPHIES

ARTRESS CORNMESSER

Artress writes fiction drawn from her many life experiences and the stories people share with her. She has undergone early pregnancy, single motherhood, the raising of her grandchildren, and the loss of loved ones, as well as seeing the success of the next generation. Her first book, *Unto the 3rd and 4th Generation*, was published in May, 2006 and well received by all who read it. *What Goes Around*, her second book, is about young love, betrayal and revenge. The personal story that appears here was shared with her dear friend, Edy Henderson, who may have had a better "bio" for Artress on her computer. The remaining editors apologize for not being able to contact Artress and for not knowing much more about her to share with our readers.

Nora J. Stone, Linda Brummett-O'Hare,
Richiko Tsuji and SuSu Martinez about the
time Richiko gave her apology.

NORA J. STONE

A product of the WWII Occupation of Japan, Nora's mother is from a family with Samurai roots and her father grew up in "Hoovervilles" in Mississippi. This bicultural perspective allowed Nora to realize that life is what you make of it. With the help of Uncle Sam she was able to complete a BA in English Literature, taking advantage of being a native speaker in the work place, when she really wanted to be a writer and artist. Google "NoraJean" and you'll find hundreds of links to her web site, which is dedicated to teaching polymer clay art online for free and featuring her short fiction. A mother to four grown sons, grandmother to three boys and a girl, sister to five women and an aunt to over a dozen of their offspring, Nora finally found time to write and create art. This will be her first published work of non-fiction and her mother thought the story was "so us." She describes herself as a "rice-cracker geek posing as a wilted flower child, Boomer granny, online art teacher who rants on a blog so as not to drive my family crazier than they already are. Main Fault: Mercury in Virgo, holding nouns hostage with too many adjectives."

EDY HENDERSON
(1945-2013)

Edy utilized her science background to write a feminist science fiction novel, so radical that she needed a pseudonym for self protection. Anyone who "Googles" Edy Henderson will discover she was an internationally recognized computer scientist who, as a strategic analyst for AOL, helped mold the direction of internet governance and protocols that power the web. A pioneer of new technologies, Edy had written articles and taught courses in computer graphics, telephony, and "How to Make $ on the Internet". She traveled to Japan and Europe to work on collaborative science projects and international standards. Edy led the development of web servers and search engines at AOL, and managed software development at Sun Microsystems, Schlumberger, and NASA. She also played violin for the San Jose Symphony, acted as Artistic Advisor for the Santa Cruz Symphony and studied Indonesian Gamelan music. As VP of DesignElevations.com, Edy oversaw website development, operations, graphics, E-commerce, Customer Support, and did some fashion modeling, while volunteering and raising funds for the American Cancer Society

and YWCA. She authored a vegan cookbook, while she and her husband enjoyed spending time with their two grown children and competing with their grandson at PlayStation. Edy's degree was in Mathematics and Spanish; and she is listed in *Who's Who of American Women*.

Edy Henderson's family (clockwise from center):
Edy's mother Grace, Sylvia's son Mark, Edy,
Marlene, Patty, Sylvia, Gracie, Alonzo, Linda.

BOBBIE HOPKINS SPIVEY

Bobbie and Mom

Bobbie is a published prize-winning author of short stories who earned her MA in Family Counseling by developing a children's workshop project combining dance, music, painting, story and sand play to encourage the appreciation of diversity and recognition of the commonality in various cultures' art forms. As a counselor and workshop presenter, she emphasized communication and discovery of each person's unique gifts. She considers her own unique gifts as just another blessing to add to that of having survived a nine-month hospital stay after a childhood accidental burning. Bobbie won a scholarship at the age of five to study piano under the tutelage of Dr. Antonia Brico; and competed in master classes with her contemporary, Judy Collins, until the age of thirteen, when Bobbie switched to voice lessons. She considers herself blessed to have had the opportunity to attend her first two years of college and live in Mexico, where the family learned the language by living it daily in a small village. From a background of ballet and modern dance, Bobbie moved into the area of ethnic dancing as a young adult, teaching interpretative movement and expanding it into liturgical dance presentations. Bobbie acknowledges the gift of her roots, from the multi-layered opportunities offered her to the legacy of believing in oneself and reaching out to others. She lives in Sacramento, California with her husband of over fifty years, proudly proclaims the accomplishments of her two adult children, and spoils her grandson, every chance she gets.

Billie Ruth Hopkins Furuichi

Billie is an Art Activist, a songwriter, a poet, a dancer, a musician and a teacher. She has been a bilingual community liaison in both Denver, Colorado and Brookings, Oregon, facilitating an original seminar series, *Angelita's Wings*, which includes a workshop for youth at risk, *Breathing Through Walls*, using the *Transformation Wheel*.™ Her work interweaves movement meditation, sacred dance, silk painting, writing haiku, original music and reframing techniques. Billie Ruth is the founder of One Society International, a non-profit organization conducting student exchange programs to Japan and the former Soviet Union, and she has organized and traveled as the youth support and leadership director on twelve of these exchanges. Her nature is to celebrate cultural differences and to mediate misunderstandings – an ability, strengthened by her twenty two-year marriage to Isamu, a Japanese Master Chef whom she met while teaching English in Japan. In addition to being a widely published poet, Billie Ruth has also developed technical training documents for maintenance of underground telephone cables, and is currently working on a new book, *When the Red Thread Breaks*. A recent widow, Billie Ruth is the Writing Center Coordinator at Crescent Valley High School in Corvallis, Oregon.

Billie and Mom

JERRINE MINKUS ROWLEY

Coming from an unhappy family situation, Jerrine's main goal in life has been to succeed in a marriage. A veteran of two failed attempts, Jerrine has been very happily married for 26 years to her husband, David. The lessons learned in such a union – mainly the ability to feel loved and be loving, to not expect criticism or be critical, to trust one another – has been the success Jerrine searched for. Majoring in Business came easy to her, and her creative outlets were ceramics, stained glass and dance. Just as she was about to begin another college program to become a medical assistant, she got "turned onto" photography, which evolved into another major and has continued to be her passion. After college, Jerrine worked at the Photography Center in San Francisco, and set up her own darkroom. Her photography studio is now a computer. Jerrine has won several prizes – most notably, first place at the Marin Humane Society Cat Photo Contest in 2003 and as "Rookie of the Year" at the Marin Photography Club in 2005. Jerrine retired in 2008 and lives with David in southern Oregon, volunteers with several organizations, and has a full life, loving to travel, read, garden, cook, and have fun with friends. She is blessed with good health and appreciates life to its fullest.

Jerrine and Mama

KATHE KOKOLIAS

Kathe is a writer and photographer living in upstate New York and Ixtapa, Mexico. She is a member of the International Women's Writing Guild, WomanWords, and Wild Women writing groups, and is a board member of the Hudson Valley Writers Guild; she also belongs to the Colonie Art League and the Art Center of the Capital Region. "Burnt Toast" and another essay aired on National Public Radio. Her essays have been selected for several issues of *Another Day in Paradise*, a magazine published in Mexico, *Inkpot*, a literary journal, the *Pyramid Lake Anthology*, the *Peer Glass Anthology*, and *Enlightening Bolt*. Her story and photos on "Day of the Dead" appeared in the Sunday travel section of the Albany *Times Union*. She has completed a memoir entitled *What Time do the Crocodiles Come Out?* about her misadventures in Mexico. Kathe received an MA in Management from John F. Kennedy University in Orinda, California. She is married and has six grandchildren.

Elizabeth French

After raising her son as a single mother, Elizabeth participated in the Women's Re-Entry program at Cabrillo College where she took writing classes, and was the recipient of the Presidents Award for her short story about a single mom raising her son in a prejudiced small town. Elizabeth married at seventeen, gave birth to a beautiful baby boy, was divorced by twenty-one, and moved to a seventh floor walk-up on Steiner Street in San Francisco, carrying her infant son on her back. She shared the apartment house with Guy Johnson (Maya Angelou's son), who taught her son music and became a lifelong friend. Elizabeth with her small son, Thomas, spent 1976 observing the bi-centennial traveling the USA by car. In trying many professions, Elizabeth was the first female Police Officer in Gillette, Wyoming. While in Minnesota in 90 degree below weather, she met a trucker who offered her a job managing his apartment complex in Pacific Grove. She is now in real estate in the Santa Cruz area.

Mom and Elizabeth

LISA SWALLOW

Lisa is a children's book writer living in Portland, Oregon. She has four grown children and three grandchildren. Writing is her addiction, her world view, her path for growth, and her livelihood. It has been the one constant in her life. Two of her adult short stories appeared in anthologies from TOR Books in the late 1980's, and her non-fiction work has appeared in several national magazines. After her divorce in 1990 she traded the fun of freelancing for the steady income of technical documentation. She's recently quit that job to write fiction, where her real passion lies. In the past two years she has completed three picture books and a young adult urban fantasy. While her fiction crosses genres, audience levels, and time, her themes always revolve around identity, belonging, acceptance, and love. Follow her at *swallowtales.net*

Lisa's Mom

CHARLA K. ROTTER

Charla was a personal friend of Edy Henderson's, one of the 'gang of pals' that periodically got together over one excuse to gather or another. Her story about her mother *does* give us a glimpse into their relationship, and we are sure that Charla has had an interesting life that we'd have been honored to share here. However, Charla asked that we not include a picture or a biography – but would allow her story to stand on its own.

ROSEANNA FRECHETTE

Roseanna is a longtime member of Denver's thriving poetry community. Former publisher of *Rosebud Forum* magazine, she has great passion for the power of small press and the beauty of spoken word. Her works have appeared in a variety of small press publications, most recently *Semicolon* out of Naropa University and *Lummox* out of L.A. Interpretive dancer and yogi as well as poet, Roseanna's performance art is informed by her natural connection to the Tao. She has studied and taught Eastern philosophy, meditation, yoga and dance as integrative practices for many years. Her performances and written works are vibrant and dynamic as she allows her voice to be heard through story, song, and poems ever-changing.

Roseanna's Mom

BETTY SANDERSON OWEN

With no distinguished degrees to hang on to her name, Betty worked as a telephone operator at a small flying school after graduation from high school. She was at her post when the news of the attack on Pearl Harbor came over the radio. It was there that she met and married a young flight instructor who would soon receive a commission in the US Naval Reserve. What followed was a whirlwind of life as the wife of a Naval Aviator. Thrust into the business of war and the flight training of recruits, and from there to the US Naval Ferry Command, they lived on war rations and in strange places, while raising their young son, Mike. Betty's creativity emerged first in learning to sew little suits for her baby made from old uniforms, and in her vivid descriptions of military life in the letters she wrote home. The war ended but the adventures continued as the military man sought his sea legs; college; teaching . . . new job in California. Home and family came first, and 3 more children followed, but there was always choir and community chorus, and somewhere there was time for lessons in china painting. Art bloomed and grew. She held classes in China Painting wherever she could get a group of ladies together. Artistic endeavors expanded to oils on canvas. A digital camera accompanied her on her long walks, and another component was added. Retirement opened new vistas, words began to fill up Betty's head, and the pages piled up and were bound into books with names like *Reflection from the Blue Bench* and *The Way We Were* . . .illustrated with photos! She is coming up on 93, and still writes, shoots and paints!

Debra Madison

Debra is a writer and artist in contemporary Haiga, the merging of a haiku and an image. The process begins when one moves from being an *observer*, to becoming an *active-participant*. It starts as *noticing* what is going on in the everyday world; paying attention to the day's surprises and focusing attention more closely than is otherwise done. It is a meditative and spiritual practice. She is also a Book  and Document Restoration Specialist, restoring maps, documents, Family Bibles, and rare books dating back 400 years. It was the understanding of the mechanics of books, combined with her writing and art background that spurred her to enter the world of Book Arts. She has been the recipient of a grant from The Sacramento Metropolitan Arts Commission, and is an award winning artist from Campbell's Soup for "The Campbell's Art of Soup" contest. Debra describes the non-traditional books she has written, designed and produced as creating housing for words, images and ideas with titles such as: *Alice Looking Through The Wonderland of Glass, Goop Tales, Anagrammatically Red, and My 42 years of mmm…mmm…*

Debra's mom

Good. Many of her creations have been exhibited throughout California and Oregon. The Sacramento Central Library has many examples of her work kept in the vault in The Sacramento Room with other rare and valuable books. Debra lives in Northern California with her husband Bill, who is also a writer and photographer.

DONNA OWEN HOPKINS ELLIS
(1919-2004)

Mother to two of the editors of this book, Donna was a much stronger woman than any of the stories in this collection tell. At the age of twelve, while babysitting her younger brother, sister and a friend of her sister's, she outsmarted a knife-wielding crazy lady who had escaped from the asylum in the next town. Single-handedly she raised awareness of an environmental threat to Colorado's pine forest to a legislative level, beginning by recruiting her Indian Hills neighbors to sighting the beetle infestation and convincing the landowners to destroy the affected trees in the proper manner. Donna always believed her husband and children

were better writers than she; but after her death many beautiful journal entries, poems and short stories were discovered belying her self-assessment. She always put others' desires and comforts before her own, showing the world her positive outlook and holding inward all her doubts and fears.

Ruth Owen Puchek
(1928-2013)

Ruth was born in Golden, CO and grew up riding horses in the hills around the town. She spent time serving in the USO during WWII in DC before going on to college where she met her husband. They both taught school in Denver, CO while she raised two boys and Joe went to Seminary. When they were called to Lanai to serve as minister to a small church, their boys were grown and Ruth returned to her passion – Art. Her sons remember her creativity – like a pillow "snowman" for Christmas in Hawaii. After Joe's death, Ruth traveled the world visiting people and places, enjoying the world "her way with any friend who said they'd join her. She didn't just teach art; she was an artist and later enjoyed working with different forms of watercolors," says one of her sons. He continued at her memorial, "Ruthie was the consummate teacher and enjoyed her students young and old. We were all her students in one way or another." She vowed to live to 85 – and almost did.

Nina Boyd Krebs, Ed.D

A psychologist for three decades, Dr. Nina Krebs also worked as a teacher – junior high through graduate school – and as an organizational consultant. She presented workshops throughout the United States related to women in the workplace and issues of cultural diversity. Publications include *Psychotheatrics: The New Art of Self-Transformation* with Rob Allen, *Changing Woman Changing Work* and *Edgewalkers: Defusing Cultural Boundaries on the New Global Frontier.* Currently, *Dramatic Psychological Storytelling* with Rob Allen, is at press at Palgrave Macmillan. Nina has embraced art-making as her main focus in retirement. Her first solo show, *Portent and Portal, the Soul and Spirit of Everywoman,* 2003, presented her mixed media work at the Kondos Gallery in Sacramento, California. Subsequently her work has been in juried shows in northern California, where she continues painting as well as creating digital and other mixed media projects. Research interests include archaeological and spiritual roots of indigenous art as it relates to universal imagery and the human condition in present time.

DEDICATION TO EDY HENDERSON
(1945 – 2013)

We gratefully acknowledge the many hours of planning and days sharing ideas the three of us spent in Edy's lovely hilltop home in Aptos, California. We had planned to have our final wrap-up in the same welcoming surroundings. Sadly, Edy and her husband were killed in their home in 2013.

Edy with her mother, father, and two older sisters

YOUR ENCOURAGEMENT

In his book *Loved Beyond Measure*, Rev. Michael T. Moran wrote:

"...I wish there were less hype about traditional motherhood and more acknowledgment of not-so-traditional 'mothers' in our midst – people who come in all colors, shapes, sizes, genders, and ages. And, more than anything, I wish there were a lot more empathy for those who suffer from not being acknowledged on Mother's Day.

"Let us honor them all on Mother's Day – women who conceived, women who bore, women who reared, women who lost, women who let go, women who made difficult choices, and people of any gender who mother and nurture others.

"This year, and in the future, in addition to giving the 'moms in your life' the gift of cards, flowers and a well-deserved meal cooked by someone else, give her the gift of peace. Offer a prayer for the end of war, terrorism and domestic violence. Be a dreamer, and imagine a future where no mother has to mourn the death a child or a loved one because of the insanity of terrorism and war. To all mothers who are fighting in wars, or whose children are fighting, or are innocently caught in the crossfire, may you experience peace, courage and hope for a peaceful world."

Moran, Michael T. *Loved Beyond Measure: Messages of Inspiration, Hope and Joy.* ©2013. Oneness Ministries, P. O. Box 60846, Sacramento, CA 95860, pp. 52-53

Your Invitation

Thank you for allowing us to come into
your space, if for just a short time. We have
been able to let go of the fear in sharing our
private moments because we have learned
from our own sharing with each other –
that sometimes the sharing promotes the
inner healing – that in allowing light to
enter into those dark secret places within, we can feel the healing energy
flow in and through the spaces – breathing a new view of how things were.

Billie and Bobbie welcome your comments and suggestions – better
yet, we welcome your own stories – for we know you have them – to be
submitted for inclusion in the next edition of *My Mother–Myself*. You
can reach us through the website: *www.mymother-myself.com*

We invite you leave a comment on our Facebook page:
www.facebook.com/My Mother–Myself

We hope that you are already finding similarities in your own stories
– or even better – discovering that "there, but for the Grace of God . . ."
yours has a better ending.

Perhaps you are sharing these stories already with your close friends
– if that is the case, invite them to read *My Mother–Myself* and maybe
you will find ideas jumping back and forth between you – maybe – you
both might want to submit stories. We would love to know if they are
submitted as a result of your own sharing.

Virtual Hugs—

May you sleep with the soft brush of angel wings on your brow.

Lightning Source UK Ltd.
Milton Keynes UK
UKHW020029160322
400107UK00010B/2429

9 781935 9145